WHAT DO I DO WHEN
TEENAGERS DEAL
WITH DEATH?

Dr. Steven Gerali

■ ZONDERVAN®

ZONDERVAN.com/
AUTHORTRACKER
follow your favorite authors

youth
specialties

ZONDERVAN

What Do I Do When Teenagers Deal with Death?
Copyright 2009 by Steve Gerali

Youth Specialties resources, 1890 Cordell Ct. Ste. 105, El Cajon, CA 92020 are published by Zondervan, 5300 Patterson Ave. SE, Grand Rapids, MI 49530.

ISBN 978-0-310-29193-0

Cover design by Invisible Creature
Interior design by Brandi Etheredge Design

Printed in the United States of America

CONTENTS

2.2 Questions That Demand Theological Consideration
2.2A Why Does God Allow Tragedy, Death, and Suffering?
2.2B Is the Dead Person in Heaven?
2.2C Should We Remove Life Support?
2.2D Is Cremation Biblically Acceptable?

2.3 Scripture Passages to Consider

3.1 Practical Help for Youth Workers

3.2 Helping a Family
3.2A Immediate Response
3.2B Helping a Terminally Ill Teenager Face Death
3.2C What's It Going to Be Like Before Death Comes?
3.2D Planning a Funeral, Memorial, or Committal Service
3.2E Sample Ceremonies

3.3 Helping Surviving Teenagers
3.3A Helping a Grieving Teenager
3.3B Debriefing a Youth Group
3.3C Positive Ways to Express Grief
3.3D Common Mistakes Youth Workers Make
3.3E Debriefing a Volunteer Staff
3.3F Miscellaneous Tips

3.4 Dealing With Personal Grief

4.1 Agencies

4.2 Online Resources

4.3 Books and Printed Materials

WHAT DO I DO WHEN... BOOK SERIES
| INTRODUCTION |
Read This First!

It's very important you read this Introduction. This series of books has grown out of years of listening to professional and volunteer youth workers wrestle through difficult ministry situations. I usually know what's coming when the conversation starts with, "What do I do when...?" Most of the time they're looking for remedial help, but many times the issues that are covered in this book series have no preventative measures available. Many of these issues aren't given serious thought until they evidence themselves in the fabric of ministry. Then youth workers, church staff, parents, and even teenagers scramble to get some kind of understanding, remedy, support, or theological perspective on the situation. This series is designed to help you.

Before we move too far ahead, you need to know a few things. First, just because you read these books and acquire some helping skills, that doesn't make you a professional counselor or caregiver. In many situations you'll need to help parents and teenagers network with professional mental health workers, medical professionals, or, in some cases, legal counsel. Oftentimes the quality of care regarding these issues lies in the rapid response of helping professionals. So if you don't get anything else out of this series, get this:

The best thing you can do as an effective helper is realize you're not a trained counselor and you must refer, refer, refer.

Second, often when youth workers are in the throes of an issue, they'll quickly access the Internet for help and information. Researching something online can be very time-consuming, and it can provide unreliable information. So this book series is designed to offer reliable information that's quickly accessible for anyone who's working with adolescents.

Third, each book follows a similar format that's designed to help you navigate the information more easily. But more importantly, it also provides a model to help you deal with the issue at hand. What Do I Do When... books are divided into the following four sections:

SECTION 1: UNDERSTANDING THE ISSUE OR "PRESENTING PROBLEM"

Each book will start with an *epistemology* of the issue—in other words, the knowledge regarding its nature and scope. Many youth workers formulate their opinions, beliefs, and ideas using faulty information that's been passed through the grapevine—often without realizing the grapevine has root rot. Faulty information can change the trajectory of our actions in such a way it actually causes us to miss the mark. And many times our "misses" can be destructive to a kid who's already struggling with a painful issue.

We cannot expect to lead a teenager to the truth of Scripture if we start with a foundation that's built upon a lie or deception. We must be informed, seeking to understand the presenting problem as learners with a teachable spirit. In some cases these books may provide only the basics about an issue. But hopefully they'll be enough to create a solid foundation that gives direction for further research from reliable sources.

SECTION 2: UNDERSTANDING HOW YOUR THEOLOGY INTERSECTS THE ISSUE OR PRESENTING PROBLEM

Each book will also cover at least one theological perspective that informs the situation. However, please note I plan to give theological insights from multiple perspectives, so you'll know the theological voices adolescents and their families hear. Some of these voices may not resonate with your particular view, but it's important you develop a gracious, loving, and understanding heart. Keep in mind you're dealing with desperate, hurting, and broken people who—in the midst of their pain and struggle—are seeking grace and hope, not someone with theological answers.

I realize there's a danger in writing like this. Whenever the playing field is leveled—in other words, when one's internalized theological framework is challenged or an opposing theological view is given—it can quickly become a fisticuffs arena to champion truth. I believe that truth brings freedom (John 8:32). But let's remember that the Pharisees believed they'd cornered the market on truth simply because they held to a rigid interpretation of the Scriptures, yet they failed to listen for God's voice in others—especially in the Messiah.

A dear friend of mine once confronted a group of students by asking, "Is your interpretation of Scripture always right?"

The students knew that if they replied affirmatively, then they'd set themselves up as the source of infallibility. So they replied, "No, nobody can be right all the time."

My friend then asked, "In what areas are you wrong?"

His wisdom during that loving confrontation helped those students see that unless they openly and graciously engaged the theological perspectives of others, they'd never know if their own perspectives were lacking. Our goal in helping kids through difficult issues is to usher Christ into their situations. Many times that may not be with answers but with presence, affection, support, and understanding.

I recall a situation in which my dear, sweet, Italian mother was hurting for a young couple who'd been caught in sexual sin (she and my dad had mentored this couple). The disciplinary actions of the church were harsh and shaming. So while the church acted in rightness, it failed to see other theological perspectives that informed this situation, such as a theology of reconciliation, grace, confession, and absolution. In my conversation with my mother, I heard her engage these things because she, too, entered into the process and pain of this young couple, and she refused to apply a static template of dealing with the issue in a "right way." Instead, she decided to deal with the issue first in a loving and good way.

It's important to remember that many times rightness is not goodness. God has called his people to be good (Matthew 5:16, Ephesians 2:10, 1 Timothy 6:17-19)—not always "right." That doesn't mean we ignore truth, nor does it mean we minimize the authority of Scripture. It just means we must be incredibly and painfully careful to err on the side of that which is loving and good. Wrestling through various theological viewpoints, even if we don't initially agree with them, will keep us in the tension of being loving and good.

SECTION 3: CONSIDERING WHAT ACTIONS WE CAN TAKE

When we understand an issue or problem, we must wrestle through the theological and consider appropriate action. That can mean anything from doing more research to aggressively seeking solutions. In this third section, I'll attempt to provide you with a framework for action, including practical examples, applications, and tips. This will only be a skeletal plan you'll need to own and tweak to fit the uniqueness of your situation. There is rarely one prescribed action for an issue—every situation is unique because of the people involved.

Throughout the years, I've watched youth workers attempt to use books about youth ministry as one uses an instruction manual for the assembly of a bicycle. They assume that if they put this screw into this hole, then this part will operate correctly. Likewise, they expect that applying a tip from a book will fix a student or situation. If only life were this easy!

Every example provided in this series of books grows out of my years of ministry and clinical experience, input from God's people, and proven results. But they're not foolproof solutions. God desires to be intimately involved in the lives of students and their families, as they trust in God through their difficult times. There is no fix-all formula—just faithfulness. So as you follow some of the directives or action steps in these books, remember that you must prayerfully seek God in the resolution of the issues.

SECTION 4: ADDITIONAL RESOURCES

In this section I'll provide some reliable resources for further help. These Internet sites, books, and organizations can assist you in mobilizing help for teenagers and their families. Hopefully this will save you many hours of hunting, so you can better invest in your students and their families.

Where needed, I'll also give a brief comment or description for the source. For example, some sources will serve to explain a different theological perspective from mainstream. This will help you to be informed before you run out and buy the book or engage the Web site.

I trust this book series will assist you in the critical care of teenagers and their families. God has put you on the front lines of attending, shepherding, and training people who are very dear and valuable to his heart. The way you respond to each person who's involved in these critical issues may have eternal consequences. My prayer is that everyone who reads these books will be empowered in a new way to usher Jesus more deeply and practically into the lives of precious teenagers.

UNDERSTANDING ADOLESCENT DEATH

| SECTION 1 |

The phone woke Pastor Dave out of a deep sleep. He squinted at the alarm clock on the bedside table—3:20 a.m. "This better not be a prank call," he muttered to his wife. The broken, tearful voice on the other end of the line jolted Dave into a sobering sense of awareness.

"Dave, this is Mark Johnson. We have some bad news. Our son Matt was in an automobile accident with some other teenagers from the youth group. They went to a restaurant after a concert. But as they were coming home, they were hit by a drunk driver. Matt is in critical condition with severe head trauma. Jared Christiansen, Lydia Michaels, and Rachel Martin were all fatally wounded. The families are coming to the hospital now. Can you meet us here?"

"I'll be right there!" Dave responded.

Fatally wounded...fatally wounded... The words rang incomprehensibly in Dave's head. As he tried to wrap his mind around it, the reality of death began to root itself in his consciousness. Three of his core students were dead—including the senior pastor's daughter—and the life of another one hung in the balance. Dave had been in youth ministry for five years, and this had never happened to him before. For a moment he stared at his wife, who waited to hear the tragic news. Dave knew teenagers weren't exempt from death, and he'd heard of death hitting other youth ministries. But he wasn't ready for it to come this close to home.

As Dave got dressed, his mind raced. He thought about what he needed to say to the parents; about stepping into leadership at the church while the senior pastor and his family grieved; about the logistics of helping families plan funerals and memorial services; the fallout and aftereffects on the youth group, school, and community; and the need to stay in control while personally feeling an incredible sense of loss, grief, and pain.

Overwhelmed, Dave finished tying his shoes, pulled on his jacket, and grabbed his car keys from the dresser. He looked over at his wife who was now sitting up in bed in a state of shock. As he walked out of the room, Dave prayed, "Lord, help me...what do I do now?"

1.1 UNEXPECTED DEATH

The most difficult and unexpected form of death is that of a teen or child. Teenagers have a sense of invincibility. And the adults around them, while they don't believe teens to be invincible, are never prepared for the death of a teenager. Most youth workers can go their entire careers without doing a funeral for a teenager. So when death comes to a youth ministry, youth leaders like Pastor Dave tend to feel ill-prepared to meet it.

We expect to outlive our parents, so the death of a parent has instinctual elements that allow us to cope with their passing. We also believe we may outlive our peers (spouse, friends, siblings). So this type of death also has some built-in coping mechanisms because of our ability to face our own mortality. But we never expect to outlive our children. The death of a child or teenager defies the natural order of the life span. And the situation becomes more traumatic because the ending of a young life is rarely the result of natural causes. So a person has to navigate not only the premature death of a teenager, but also the tragedy and trauma that took the teen's life.

Accidental death by motor vehicle crashes is the leading cause of death among American youth between the ages of 15 and 20, accounting for approximately 40 percent of all fatalities in this age bracket.[1] Other causes include death by accident (nontraffic), homicide, suicide, drug and substance overdose, and illness or disease.

While the accidental death of a teenager hits a youth group hard, there are other aspects and types of death a youth worker may encounter. Death may invade your youth ministry when a teen loses a parent or someone else she's close to. It may even affect a youth ministry before the death occurs, such as when a teenager is diagnosed with a terminal disease. However, while still tragic, this situation usually allows people to prepare for death, so the dynamic of this process is very different from that of an accidental death.

Intended to serve as a quick guide to help youth workers navigate the complexities of death, this book will deal with the forms of death and bereavement that surround adolescents and their families. We'll look at ways to—

- Debrief a youth group when a teenager dies
- Help a church and grieving family make the necessary preparations

- Prepare teens for what they may see, feel, and experience throughout the grieving process
- Help teens whose parent or other loved one is facing death by a terminal disease
- Deal with our own personal grief as youth workers

Additionally, we'll try to understand a theology of death that can inform the way we respond to teens and their questions. And we'll search for a solution to Pastor Dave's unspoken question: *What do I do when death comes?*

1.2 ACCIDENTAL DEATH

This is the most common way teenagers die. And the trauma of death is compounded by the overwhelming shock of tragedy and its unexpectedness. The horror of accidental death leaves us feeling helpless and searching for ways this could have been prevented. And, unfortunately, we usually come to some conclusions about our physical limitations and mortality, realizing there are no preventative measures.

Oftentimes the next logical step will be to question God—the only One who could have prevented this. Later in the book, we'll address the theological questions that accompany death.

1.2A AUTOMOBILE-RELATED DEATH

While there are no preventative measures we can take against accidental death, there are some precautionary measures we can follow. Statistics regarding the accidental death of teenagers are sobering. The National Highway Traffic Safety Administration (NHTSA) has released the following information:[2]

- The leading cause of death among adolescents between the ages of 15 and 20 is motor-vehicle-related.

- While drivers between the ages of 15 and 20 account for fewer than 7 percent of the licensed drivers in the United States, they're responsible for more than 20 percent of the nation's traffic fatalities. Nearly a third of those fatalities are alcohol-related.

- More than 8,000 people are killed annually in teenage driving accidents, almost half of those being the teenage driver, a quarter of them being teenage passengers, and another quarter being the drivers of other vehicles or pedestrians killed by a teenage driver. That means approximately 6,000 teenagers die in automobile accidents.

- Teenage drivers account for the age category with the most drivers involved in alcohol-related traffic accidents.

- The National Survey on Drug Use and Health reported that most late adolescents who drive under the influence of alcohol and other drugs are under the legal drinking age of 21.

- The fatality rate of drug- and alcohol-related teen driving accidents is compounded by the fact that intoxicated teens are less likely to wear safety belts. Anywhere from 60 percent to 75 percent of the teenage drivers and passengers killed in alcohol- or drug-related driving fatalities are unrestrained.

- Other teenage traffic fatalities involve distracted teenage drivers. Teenagers seem to view their cars as "mobile apartments," complete with music (and, in some cases, video), telephone, food, and friends. Their heightened desire for adventure and their underdeveloped perceptions of danger can create a fatal formula.

1.2B DEATH-DEFYING GAMES
One form of accidental teenage death that's recently emerged in the media involves choking games. The Centers for Disease Control and Prevention (CDC) refers to this as "unintentional strangulation." Sometimes called blackout, the scarf game, space monkey, gasper, or suffocation roulette, the game gives thrill-seeking kids a buzz without the use of drugs.[3] Adolescents play these games believing the risk is minimal compared with using an illegal substance.

G.A.S.P. (Games Adolescents Shouldn't Play) is an international nonprofit educational campaign (established by the families of choking-game victims) that raises the awareness and prevention of teenage choking games. According to the G.A.S.P. Web site, it's been estimated that between 500 and 1,000 teenagers accidentally die each year as a result of playing various forms of the choking game.[4] And the numbers could be even higher, but no one knows for sure because many of these deaths are reported as suicides instead of accidental deaths. (More on this in a bit.)

In any case, the CDC intimates that choking games are on the rise. "The earliest choking-game death was identified as occurring in 1995. Three or fewer deaths occurred annually during 1995–2004; however, 22 deaths occurred in 2005, and 35 in 2006."[5]

Teenage guys more commonly engage in this practice, which often occurs at parties, in locker rooms, after sporting events (wrestlers do it and call it the "sleeper move"), or any other venue where masculine bravado is displayed. It involves a willing candidate who squats or bends over and self-induces hyperventilation. When this occurs, the candidate then quickly stands upright and holds his breath. Immediately another person puts pressure against his chest or cuts off his air supply by constricting his trachea (strangulation) until the candidate passes out. Blackout usually occurs quickly, and the candidate (in most cases) begins breathing immediately. This starts the brain oxygenating again. A few seconds after the blackout, the candidate revives and experiences a euphoric daze that gets a laugh out of his buddies and gives him his desired buzz.

The euphoria of the experience is caused by cerebral hypoxia, a condition in which the brain is deprived of oxygen but still has adequate blood flow. If cerebral hypoxia is prolonged, it can cause seizure, coma, brain death or trauma, and physical death. Unfortunately, some guys don't revive. And the fatality rate increases again when alcohol is involved.

Another variation of this phenomenon is autoerotic asphyxia. It's the same practice, only the guy uses a ligature on himself and cuts off the oxygen supply while masturbating. The cerebral hypoxia creates a euphoria that heightens the orgasmic experience during ejaculation. A guy may often use a belt, rope, scarf, or similar item with one end tied to a bedpost (or another anchored area) and the other around his neck. As he's about to reach orgasm, he may slide off the bed and allow himself to be strangulated, thinking he can (and often does) release himself before he loses consciousness. It only takes one time when consciousness is lost and the victim cannot escape the stranglehold—and the result is death.

These deaths are often reported as suicides, rather than accidental deaths. This type of "suicide" is shaming to many families because the topic of masturbation, let alone autoerotic asphyxia, isn't talked about in church. Therefore, it's easier for some families to explain this death as a suicide, rather than a choking game.

This death is also very confusing to the people who know the teenager because they never saw any signs that typically precede a suicide. Families may avoid answering questions about the signs and symptoms because they don't want to explain what really happened. As more of these deaths are reported, officials are starting to categorize them as accidental, rather than suicide, thus raising the awareness of choking games.

We shouldn't sit back and view these choking-game deaths with precautionary eyes, but rather with a preventative perspective.

We must educate students and their parents about the dangers of these activities. The CDC has published a list of warning signs that indicate that an adolescent may be engaging in some form of recreational strangulation. These include:[6]

- Verbal cues—talking about choking games, sexual euphoria, head rush, or the use of game terms (e.g., "sleeper move," "gasper," "space monkey")
- Bloodshot eyes
- Frequent complaints of severe headaches
- Marks on the neck
- Wearing high-necked shirts, even in warm weather
- Disorientation after spending time alone
- Increased and uncharacteristic irritability or hostility
- Ropes, scarves, and belts tied to bedroom furniture or doorknobs or found knotted on the floor
- The unexplained presence of items such as dog leashes, choke collars, scarves, neckties, and bungee cords
- Pinpoint bleeding spots under the skin of the face, especially the eyelids, or the lining of the eyelids, and eyes

Drinking games are another type of death-defying game that can be fatal. A drinking game requires players to drink a certain amount of alcohol in a limited period of time. These games usually range from taking a shot of liquor (usually vodka because it's odorless and looks like water, which camouflages it from adults) every time a word is mentioned in a song, to using formalized drinking board games. In 2007, two major retail chains banned the sale of drinking board games in their stores and online because of the protests by concerned people who realized the hazardous effects of such games.[7] Drinking games aren't necessarily gone, as an Internet search will yield countless drinking games that don't require the purchase of any board.

With drinking games, the consumption of alcohol is faster than the effect. This binge drinking can render an alcohol overdose long before the player passes out. The competitive edge of these games, along with the cheers and laughter of spectator friends, makes alcoholic consumption greater than if a person were just drinking socially. Usually the loser is the person who does something stupid, gets sick, or passes out.

Many times the person who becomes ill or passes out is taken by friends to a place where she can sleep off the effects of the game. This mythical cure—along with the myths of drinking coffee to sober up, walking off inebriation, or taking a cold shower—won't work. The only thing that works is for the body to purge itself of the alcohol or to receive medical treatment for the condition with careful monitoring, oxygen therapy, intravenous fluids, and some vitamins.

Reversing the effects of alcohol takes time, and drinking games may rob the individual of that very commodity. The common practice of letting a friend sleep it off (usually allowing the others to go back to their partying) puts an individual in a deeper incoherent state. While friends believe inebriation is being slept off, the individual may actually be falling deeper into a state of alcohol poisoning, because the blood alcohol concentration continues to rise even after the person stops drinking.

Alcohol poisoning, when unmonitored and untreated, can be fatal.[8]

- It causes respiratory depression. Breathing is greatly impaired or ceases because the respiratory center of the brain is poisoned by alcohol. The teen's breathing will become irregular (no consistent time between breaths) and shallow (fewer than 8 to 10 breaths a minute).

- It can depress the nervous system. This interferes with the control of involuntary muscles, such as those muscles that cause the gag reflex, which keeps a person from choking. Thus, an individual can aspirate his vomit and asphyxiate. In other words, the person drowns or suffocates in his own vomit.
- It can cause the heart, another involuntary muscle, to beat irregularly and even stop.
- It can cause dehydration, due to the continual vomiting, which can be fatal if left untreated.
- It can cause hypothermia (low body temperature), which becomes visible when the person's skin becomes pale, clammy, or bluish in color.
- It can cause seizures, unconsciousness, and coma. If the person is in a semiconscious stupor or completely unconscious and cannot be roused, the risk of death becomes greater.

Youth workers can take a preventative stance on this issue as well, by educating teenagers and their parents about the dangers of playing drinking games. Teens must also be taught to look for the warning signs and to mobilize help if a friend becomes incoherent as the result of drinking.

1.2C RISKY BEHAVIORS LEADING TO DEATH

Accidental death can also occur among teenagers due to foolish acts or inattentiveness. You may have heard of incidents where teenagers lost their lives because of some foolish action, such as diving into a swimming pool from the roof of a house, or trying to jump into the open car of a passing freight train, or following through on a dare to drink a whole bottle of Jack Daniels. While these dares and stunts are often similar to death-defying games, they're not categorized as such. Teenagers tend to take unwarranted risks. And this risk-taking behavior is the result of three developmental factors happening within the teenager.

Teens are in a cognitive stage in which their minds are transitioning from concrete to abstract thought processes. That means they don't always have the foresight (or experience) to see the potential hazards associated with their actions. Oftentimes teenagers are too caught up in the moment, and they only see their friends egging them on. This is concrete. But they fail to exercise those thought processes that engage long-term cause and effect (the abstract). This is why astonished parents will often ask their teenagers, "*What* were you thinking?" In truth—they weren't.

Adolescence is a time of great physiological change, as a teenager's body is on hormonal overload. The adrenal gland produces the hormones needed for physical and sexual maturation. It also secretes the adrenaline that puts a teenager in a state of hyperarousal when confronted with a risky activity. (Hyperarousal is a physical state when the heart rate and blood flow increase, respiration heightens, and physical performance peaks, among other things.) In addition, the endocrine system produces endorphins, which raise the pain threshold and lessen the level of fear that's typically associated with taking risks. Some believe testosterone also affects the aggressive risk-taking behavior in guys. While there's evidence that may support this, there's nothing conclusive to make this statement factual. Needless to say, this entire hormonal cocktail plays strategically into the mix that yields teenage risk-taking behavior.

The last part of the brain to develop in teenagers is the prefrontal cortex. This part of the brain is responsible for judgment. Calculating the risk and whether the warranted action is a sound decision may be lacking in teens. Without the full development of this area of the brain (which is usually completed in a person's mid-twenties), teens will lack good judgment and engage in more risks. By the way, the prefrontal cortex matures earlier in girls than it does in guys. This may be another factor to explain why guys are more likely to engage in risky, death-defying behaviors than girls are.

Teenagers have a sense of invincibility. Their own mortality is often too abstract for them to grasp, and their lack of judgment makes them miscalculate (overestimate) their own abilities. Therefore, teenagers tend not to believe they could die while engaging in these behaviors. Teens are often sobered—after the fact—by the death of a teenage friend or acquaintance.

While these physiological factors play into the configuration that leads to adolescent risk-taking, it doesn't mean adults shouldn't warn teenagers ("They can't help themselves!"); nor does it mean we can prevent their accidental deaths. The best thing we can do is *not* affirm risky behaviors as merely feats of good adventure. When teenagers excitedly share their war stories about drag racing, cliff jumping, etc, we must take a sobering approach and not give any hint the behavior was acceptable. We need to speak authoritatively into the lives of our students by talking through judgment issues. This exercise will help stimulate their teenage brains in a way that will help them grow. It will also expose them experientially to insights they wouldn't normally have because of their age and immaturity.

1.2D UNSAFE ENVIRONMENTS THAT CAUSE DEATH
This type of accidental death is often very devastating to a church, youth ministry, or parachurch organization. It typically involves some tragic experience that occurs outside the control of adult

overseers—even when there is careful attentiveness. Death in this fashion is quick, and it can often be avoided. Many times safety measures are overlooked because the youth worker or organization believes death can't happen at a ministry activity. This naïveté, accompanied by a sense of invincibility, can disqualify a person or organization from working with minors and add years of trauma to many lives. Some examples of this type of death follow:

Drowning. Teenagers can get caught in tide currents, trapped under a raft or boat, and so on—even when lifeguards are present.

Electrocution. I heard about an incident at a church-owned camp, where a lamppost on the pier, located right at the water line, had become corroded over time. The resulting hole in the post sent an electrical current through the water surrounding it. So when a group of students went down to the pier and a girl sat and put her feet into the water—she was immediately electrocuted.

Death by Prop. A youth worker accidentally shot and killed himself when he used a gun as a prop for a sermon illustration. He didn't realize a bullet was in the chamber of the gun. These types of risky illustrations can often turn fatal, in this case to the preacher, but also to a student.

Falls and Blunt Trauma. During camps or retreats, students have fallen from mountainous overhangs, buildings, and trees, resulting in their death. Teenagers have even lost their lives on ski trips because they overestimate their abilities.

Crushing. Some youth groups have experienced the trauma of losing a student who was crushed to death at a sporting event or concert as the result of an out-of-control crowd or a victory riot.

When the accidental death of a teenager occurs because of the lack of proper safety precautions, it has an added psychological effect on teens, parents, and those who work in the organization. Teens and adults may feel as though their trust in the person or organization in charge has been violated. The person in charge may also feel a great deal of culpability and guilt, possibly without warrant. Safety issues often require an investigation of negligence. In some cases criminal charges and liability may follow. For the person in charge, and those in the organization who love teenagers and have devoted their lives to youth ministry, this is devastating and shaming, heaping trauma upon trauma. In a litigious society, care and safety must be intentional and profiled. While this may not prevent accidental death, it can eliminate added tragedy.

Some steps could include—
Strictly Enforced Rules. Teenagers tend to horse around a lot, and they don't usually consider the potentially fatal consequences. Rules that have safety implications must be written out, verbally stated, and strictly adhered to. Youth workers may be afraid a teen won't return to the youth ministry if the rules are strictly enforced. Youth workers might also believe that teens will think they're over-reacting, so the rules aren't enforced. It only takes one wrong trajectory to make a situation fatal. Imagine the one time an accident does occur and a teen dies. I've heard many people express regret they weren't stricter regarding safety issues. Understandably, the enforcement of safety rules won't prevent all accidents from happening, but it will convey a strong precautionary message to youth and their families. In addition, it speaks volumes about your love and value for the well-being of teens, even if they don't recognize the importance right now.

Safety Checks. Many organizations are required by law to have safety checks regarding facilities and equipment. Churches that own camps or retreat facilities cannot neglect or overlook these precautions. Youth workers should ask questions about the safety of facilities and the frequency of their inspection. If responses are tentative or unsatisfactory, a youth worker should refuse to take kids into that setting until there is a proper inspection.

Adult Leader Involvement. I've noticed that free time at camps and retreats often means "you can do anything you want while the staff catches a nap" time. Leadership should keep tabs on students' whereabouts and activities at all times. This is why an 8:1 ratio (eight students to one adult leader) is an effective safety measure. In general, it's important to note that the riskier the activity, the more leadership is needed. For example, if you're rafting with your youth group, you should consider a 4:1 ratio (students to adult leader).

Stop Dangerous Activities. Many times youth workers allow their fear of not being liked by teens to interfere with safety issues. If students are engaging in activities that have an element of danger, which could result in injury or death, leaders must stop it. There can be no allowance for students who plead, "Just one more time!" Remember, you become the voice of reason to people who may be lacking it.

1.3 ILLNESS LEADING TO DEATH

The 2004 Journal of Pediatrics estimated there are about 3,000 teenagers who die from terminal illnesses every year.[9] Given that number a youth ministry is not exempt from facing the death of a terminally ill teenager. Some youth ministries have faced the devastating results of a terminal illness. While difficult, there is often less psychological trauma than there is to accidental death. Terminal illness can hit a youth ministry in two different ways. The first and most traumatic is the death of a student because of disease. The second is when a student's parent or other loved one dies from a disease.[9]

A terminal illness is an incurable disease with the end result of death. While that's a technical definition, a patient may not be labeled "terminally ill" unless the disease is advanced and there's less than six months' life expectancy left. It's during this time doctors usually advise the family to get their affairs in order. This prepares them for the inevitable because curative treatment is no longer effective, meaning there's nothing more that can be done medically.

Once it's been determined that medical treatment of the disease is no longer effective, the patient and family are often consulted regarding their desires for the next phase of care. This can be very difficult for the family, the teen, and everyone involved. It may require the family to wrestle through advance directives, such as giving orders not to resuscitate, stopping life support, quitting chemotherapy, choosing hospice care, and so on. These difficult decisions force people to process how their theology intersects and informs their choices and actions. (We'll deal with this topic a bit more in the next section of this book.)

In addition, a family may be faced with decisions like bringing the teenager home to die. Most people who face a terminal disease, including teenagers, want to die at home. Being in familiar surroundings brings a sense of comfort and security. It also allows for an environment in which visitors can come and go regularly. While company is often good for the dying teenager and welcomed by the family, it can take its toll. Many times families are so engaged in wanting their teen to have fullness and quality of life in their final months they don't realize they've had a hectic flow of visitors pass through their doors. After the teenager dies, families may feel abandonment or peace once that stream of visitors dries up. Youth workers need to be aware their continued contact with the family after the loss of a teenager is a necessary ministry.

When a terminally ill patient is diagnosed as such, the treatment plan shifts from being curative to palliative. Palliative care is treatment that works to assure the best quality of life for a teenager and his family. This may involve everything from pain and symptom management to home health provisions and hospice care. The goal of palliative care is to keep the patient as comfortable as possible for as long as he's alive. Quality palliative care deals with not only the physiological issues, but also the emotional and mental health issues, spiritual concerns, and pastoral care.

1.3A TYPES OF TERMINAL ILLNESS THAT AFFECT TEENAGERS

Before we get any farther into this section, let's start with a threefold understanding:

First, any disease, infection, or illness can have a fatal effect if not properly cared for or if complications arise. The human body is very resilient, but it's also very frail. We tend to believe that teens are more resilient than their elders, which may be true—but they're still mortal. So categorizing terminal illnesses can become more difficult when we understand that a teenager could die from a bee sting.

The second thing we must understand is that while a terminal illness is incurable, not all incurable diseases have fatal outcomes.

An incurable disease that doesn't have an imminent fatal consequence is called a "chronic disease." Chronic illness is a long-term treatable but incurable illness. Examples of chronic illness include asthma and diabetes. A person may suffer with a chronic illness all her life, but it may not be the ultimate cause of her death. Chronic illnesses aren't contagious, they can sometimes be genetically passed, and they can impair the quality of life.

Third, a person can have a disease that's incurable and non-chronic and live for a long time. Curative treatment can slow the effects of the disease or retard its movement into advanced stages. These treatments can put the patient into remission (absence of activity) or remittance (a temporary abatement, without the cessation of clinical symptoms). This is why it's so difficult to find a list of terminal diseases that affect teenagers. A disease isn't labeled "terminal" unless curative treatments are no longer effective and doctors believe the patient has less than six months to live.

Keeping these things in mind, it's still important for youth workers to have an understanding of the diseases that can have a terminal effect on teenagers.

Leukemia. This is a form of cancer that affects blood cells. The normal process by which the body produces healthy new cells, which then grow old and die, is often disrupted by the production of cancer cells. Blood cells are formed in the bone marrow. In their immature state, the developing blood cells are called "stem cells" and "blasts." The stems and blasts develop into either white blood cells that help the body fight infection, red blood cells that oxygenate the tissues in the body, or platelets that help the blood coagulate and control bleeding. When blood cells mature, they move into the blood vessels. When a person has leukemia, cancer, or lymphoid, stem cells and blasts produce abnormal white blood cells that crowd out the normal cells and hinder their effectiveness.

There are different types of leukemia, typed by how rapidly the disease develops and the type of blood cell most affected. The cause of leukemia isn't known, but there are various types of treatment, including chemotherapy, radiation therapy, and bone marrow transplant.

General symptoms of leukemia:

- Anemia—having ineffective red blood cells leaves the person tired, pale, weak, and easily bruised or quick to bleed. Sores on the skin and eyes may develop.
- Fever and nausea
- Bone and joint pain—caused by the overcrowding of cells produced in the marrow
- Recurrent infections and illnesses from a weakened immune system
- Swollen and painful lymph nodes—the lymph nodes filter blood impurities, but when the abnormal white cells collect there, they cause the nodes to swell. Lymph nodes are located under the arms, in the neck, chest, and groin. Guys may experience soreness and swelling of their testicles.
- Frequent headaches
- Abdominal pain and distress—the kidney, liver, and spleen may become enlarged as a result of leukemia cells collecting there. This may also cause appetite and weight loss.
- Confusion, seizures, and loss of muscle control
- Dyspnea (labored breathing) and shortness of breath—again, caused by the clumping of leukemia cells. It can also cause coughs, wheezing, and painful breathing. Dyspnea becomes very pronounced when death is imminent.

Cancer. Cancer affects cell growth. Normal cells grow and divide. When they become old or damaged, they die and new cells are produced. This delicate process keeps a body healthy and growing. But cancer disrupts this delicate process by producing mutant cells that grow out of control and invade other tissues in the body, or metastasize. This is why breast cancer or colon cancer can spread throughout the body. In addition, the cancer cells don't die when they should, so they can clump together to form a tumor.

A cancer bears the name of the type of cell or the place where the cancer originated. Treatment varies due to the type and stage of the cancer. It can be very intense and toxic (due to the radiations and chemotherapies used), as well as life-altering. Not all cancers are fatal, but some can be life-threatening. Cancer in teenagers is rare and can usually be cured if caught in time. In some cases teenagers with cancer can lose the battle and succumb to death.

While there are more than 200 types of cancer and a few that rarely affect teenagers, three categories usually evidence themselves in adolescents who do contract cancer. These are—

- Lymphoma: A type of cancer that affects the immune system
- Melanoma: A type of cancer that begins in the *melanocytes*, or pigmented tissue. This cancer is present in moles, skin pigment, and pigmented tissue in the eyes or intestines.
- Germ cell tumors: Germ cells are cells that make up the organs responsible for germinating life. This would include sperm and egg cells and the organs of the reproductive system. While germ cell tumors largely appear in the sexual organs, they can also arise in the abdomen and pelvis, the brain, and in some cases the *mediastinum*, or midchest cavity. Some germ cell tumors, like testicular cancer, are most common in younger males between the ages of 15 and 35. It's essential that this type of cancer be detected early; otherwise it can be terminal.

Cystic Fibrosis (CF). This is a genetically inherited chronic disease that affects the endocrine glands. In a person with CF, these glands produce abnormal amounts of thick mucus that blocks the ducts affecting the pancreas, liver, and, more commonly, the lungs. The mucus in the lungs can lead to lung infection, progressive lung damage, and ultimately respiratory infection. Most often this disease is diagnosed when the patient is an infant or child, and then treatment begins.

The main goal of treatment is to maintain the function of the lungs and control or prevent lung infection. Nutritional supplements and enzyme replacement therapy can help lessen the effect of this disease on other organs. Treatment can be aggressive, costly, and time-consuming. It's also a lifelong process. Therefore, it often becomes the identity of the family, in that treatment is the focal point of all family decisions and activity planning.

Prior to the 1980s, most children diagnosed with CF didn't live past their teenage years. Due to greater medical advancements, the CF Foundation Patient Registry yielded data in 2005 that suggested the median life span for a person diagnosed with cystic fibrosis today is about 36 years old.[10]

The developmental stages of adolescence can threaten the sustained health of someone with CF. Teenagers are attempting to formulate their own identity, develop some sense of autonomy, and make significant cognitive shifts, which is difficult enough when you don't have a life-threatening disease. The teen with CF must learn to manage his own treatment plans, avoid behaviors that could affect his health (such as inhaling water while swimming in a lake, coming in contact with someone who is ill, etc.), be disciplined enough to adhere to lengthy treatment schedules, shift from pediatric care to adult care, and so on. All of this makes a significant impact on the teen's identity and on the advancement of the disease.

For example, a teen may have seen a pediatric specialist for years. The treatment is rigorous, and it consumes most of the child's (and parents') time—enzyme treatments, regulation of medications, and some form of airway clearance about four times a day. As the child ages and attempts to move into a more independent life stage, she may find it difficult to transition to another medical professional, despite her desire to do so. Seeing a pediatrician reminds her she's still a child. The need for and involvement of parents in the treatment process also serves as a reminder she isn't fully autonomous.

Teens with CF can't do many of the things their peers can do ,because they're consumed with the care and treatment of the disease. In addition, CF causes respiratory and digestive problems, which can delay physical growth and sexual development, making teens even more body-conscious than their peers and ultimately affecting teens self-esteem and social dynamics.

Milder forms of CF may not be detected until a person reaches his teenage years. And many times the effects of the disease grow worse and treatment must be increased.

General symptoms of cystic fibrosis can include—

- Frequent lung infections and pneumonia
- Extremely salty sweat
- Wheezing and coughing up thick mucus or blood
- Sinus infections and nasal polyps

- *Hyperglycemia,* or high blood sugars, which cause constant thirst and urination, blurred vision, a loss of concentration, and eventually cardiac arrhythmia and coma
- Inability to gain weight despite normal food consumption
- Foul-smelling, light-colored, bulky bowel movements or diarrhea due to improper digestion of food
- Intestinal obstruction that causes pain and vomiting
- Delayed physical growth and sexual development. In males this can cause infertility, and in females it can complicate fertility.

Sickle-Cell Anemia. This is another genetic disorder that affects the blood cells. A person with sickle-cell anemia inherits a sickle-cell gene from each parent who carries the sickle-cell trait but is asymptomatic. That means each parent must be a carrier of this recessive gene and pass it on to the child. As a result, one child in a family may have sickle-cell anemia, while other children in the same family do not. The children in the family who inherit only one recessive gene become carriers of the sickle-cell trait, while the child who inherits both recessive genes has sickle-cell anemia. Sickle-cell anemia affects mostly families of African descent and some people of Middle Eastern and Central American ethnicity.

Sickle-cell anemia affects the formation of red blood cells. Normally the cells are round, and they contain hemoglobin that carries oxygen to the body's organs and removes carbon dioxide to be exhaled by the lungs. However, the red cells in a person with sickle-cell anemia don't produce enough hemoglobin. As a result, the cells take on a "C," or sickle (crescent), shape. This causes the cells to become sticky, clump together, and block arteries and small capillaries in the joints and limbs. Sickle cells carry less oxygen than other blood cells, and they can break apart easily, creating more blockages. Sickle cells also die faster (one-sixth the life span of a normal red blood cell). Since the bone marrow can't make red blood cells fast enough to replenish the dying ones, the person is left in an anemic state.

While there is no cure for sickle-cell anemia, medical treatments can minimize the physical complications and keep death at bay. Treatment must be continuous and lifelong. It involves supplementing the body with folic acid, which is used to assist the bone marrow in the production of red blood cells. Other treatment options include the management of symptoms and minimizing the frequency of sickle-cell crisis—a very painful episode that can ravage the body with sudden acute and debilitating pain. A sickle-cell crisis can last anywhere from hours to days, but it could also cause chronic or consistent pain that lasts for months. The frequency of these crises vary from person to person, with some experiencing a crisis only annually, while others experience them monthly or more. The option of a bone marrow transplant is often considered, and many teenagers with this disorder must receive frequent blood transfusions.

The general symptoms of sickle-cell anemia include—

- Anemia, leaving the teen fatigued, pale, weak, and easily bruised
- Bone and joint pain
- Frequent infections
- Respiratory problems that can range from shortness of breath to pneumonia or other infections
- Abdominal pain from an enlarged spleen, which filters the blood. Blood can become trapped in the spleen, leading to severe anemia, and the spleen can eventually cease functioning.
- Delayed growth and puberty
- Eye problems, including a weak retina and blindness, because the membrane in the eye doesn't get enough blood

- Leg sores and ulcers. This occurs more often in guys than girls, and its cause is unclear.
- Stroke
- Rapid heart rate and hypertension
- Jaundice and liver problems
- Priapism in males, which is a painful, prolonged, and unwanted erection that causes the blood to become trapped in the penis. This can lead to impotence and may damage the penis.
- Acute chest syndrome caused by sickle cells becoming trapped in the lungs. This is similar to pneumonia and can cause infections. This syndrome becomes life-threatening.
- Multiple organ failure

Acquired Immune Deficiency Syndrome (AIDS). It's rare that a youth ministry would experience the death of a student due to AIDS, but it may feel the impact of a student who loses a loved one to AIDS. Either way, youth workers need to understand this devastating illness. Teenagers believe they're invincible and immune to the risk of getting HIV (human immunodeficiency virus). Yet data collected in 2005 by the Centers for Disease Control and Prevention indicate that the number of teenagers contracting the virus is rising.[11] So while a youth ministry may not experience a teenager dying of AIDS, they could certainly come in contact with students who have HIV. The HI-virus doesn't have a susceptibility curve, meaning healthy, strong teenagers aren't exempt from contracting it.

A person is said to have HIV when the virus enters the blood system. When the virus begins destroying the person's immune system, resulting in the body's inability to fight off disease and infection, then the person is said to have AIDS. This means a teenager can contract HIV and go for as many as 9 or 10 years without it moving into the latter stages of the disease, known as AIDS.

Therefore, many teenagers can contract HIV and not experience the illness or the deadly effects of AIDS until years later. This is one reason why we see few teenage deaths from AIDS, but we can often encounter teens who have HIV.

Here's how it works: When HIV enters a person's system, it attacks the white blood cells, which are responsible for fighting infection in the body. The HI-virus slowly attaches itself to the CD4 or T-cell and begins to replicate itself in that cell. The T-cell is usually responsible for activating the body's attack on illness and infection. In this case the HI-virus isolates that particular white blood cell to serve as its host. The CD4 cells then burst, releasing more of the newly reproduced HI-virus into the system until, over time, the person's entire immune system is useless. The CD4 cells also fight off certain cancers that invade the human body. But with the decrease in the numbers of this infection-fighting cell, the body becomes susceptible to cancer. When the immune system succumbs to HIV, the body moves into the later, or advanced stage, known as AIDS.

There is no cure for HIV/AIDS, but there are drugs called anti-retroviral drugs or protease inhibitors that slow down the reproduction of HIV and delay the development of AIDS. New drugs called "fusion inhibitors" make it difficult for the HI-virus to attach itself to the T-cells. These drugs are costly, and they don't cure AIDS. They just slow its arrival. The end result of AIDS is death. Youth workers need to understand this disease and be aware that some churches aren't accepting of those suffering from HIV and AIDS. While almost all terminal illnesses can be openly discussed, HIV/AIDS carries with it a stigma and secretiveness that isolates families. As a result, many people with AIDS die alone.

1.3B THE PSYCHODYNAMIC OF A TERMINAL ILLNESS

We've just seen how the most common terminal illnesses that affect teens have a genetic link that can be detected early in life. Therefore, many teenagers who suffer from a terminal illness may have been fighting the disease for most of their lives. In addition, a teenager may fight a nongenetic illness that progresses to a terminal state. Whatever the case, there comes a point when the ongoing treatment of the illness loses its effectiveness. Teens who face death may exhibit some of the following traits:

Teens may want more information. Adolescents have the cognitive ability to understand death, so they may have a number of questions regarding the quality of their care, the pathology of their illness, and many other issues.

Teens may romanticize death or become obsessed with it. They may begin planning their funerals, writing their wills, and constantly talking about their death. This often makes others uncomfortable.

Teens may exhibit sharp mood swings. Emotional ups and downs are all part of the processing of and coming to terms with their own death.

Teens' sleep may be disrupted. They could be worrying or they may view sleep as being an infringement on the amount of time they have left.

Teens may lack concentration.

Teens may experience "anticipatory grief." This is a form of grief that mourns the loss of life before death. Many times this is experienced with other teens, rather than with adults.

Teens may experience a sense of powerlessness and lack of control. This is magnified by the fact that teenagers are in a life stage in which they're constantly trying to gain autonomy.

Teens may develop an attitude of entitlement, rebellion, or apathy. This new demeanor is usually defined by an "I'm going to die soon" outlook.

Teens may engage in risky behaviors. Figuring they have nothing to lose, teenagers may participate in activities such as drug and alcohol experimentation, death-defying games, and other risky activities.

Teenagers may exhibit suicide ideation.

Teens may question, doubt, or attempt to clarify their spiritual beliefs.

1.3C EFFECT OF TERMINAL ILLNESS ON FAMILIES AND TEENAGERS
A terminal illness tends to become a family's identity, as their dynamic, actions, events, finances, and conversations primarily revolve around the illness. This can go on for years, causing stresses and strains to the family, creating an ever-present emotional roller coaster, and finally leaving a family without an identity at the death of the teenager. Understand that families who face imminent death often experience the following:

Financial Strain. With any terminal illness, there will be mounting medical bills that aren't covered by insurance or other medical aid. The financial burden may increase further when a parent or other caregiver must quit their jobs to care for the terminally ill teen.

Total Dependence. As the illness progresses, the dying teen becomes more dependent on his family, and the family members must rise to meet the mounting demands of personal care, which includes everything from feeding the patient to caring for his hygiene.

End-of-Life Decisions. Families will have to evaluate and make critical decisions about the different types of care, service, and treatment for the terminal patient. Everything from home health care nurses to hospice care can fall into this category. This process can often be very time intensive and emotionally draining. Many times families are encouraged to involve their teen in the decision-making process, which can make the dynamic either more difficult or easier.

Advance Directives. Families also must deal with ethical and spiritual dilemmas in their decision making when they're forced to decide about advance directives in the death process. They may have to sign papers that allow doctors to issue Do Not Resuscitate (DNR) orders, take a child off life support, or cease all life-sustaining treatments. Families in these situations will find that other people can't relate to the pain and trauma, spiritual difficulty, or unnaturalness of having to make these kinds of decisions.

1.4 HOMICIDE AND SUICIDE

After accidental death, homicide and suicide are the second- and third-leading causes of death among teenagers. And homicide is the leading cause of death among African American teens.[12] Most frequently, teenage homicides are caused by guns. When adolescents are killed in violent acts, the trauma and tragedy of the act affects the community.

1.4A TEENAGE HOMICIDES
Teen homicide can be the result of a number of factors.

Gang-Related Activity. Not all teens who die in gang-related activity were members of gangs. Many times teens are merely innocent bystanders or just in the wrong place at the wrong time.

An Impulsive Assault. Out-of-control teenage anger coupled with immature cognitive judgment can be a formula that turns an act of aggression into a homicide.

Acts of Vengeance. The epidemic of teenage mass murders experienced in the '80s and '90s was the result of disturbed and troubled teens who were pushed to the edge, resulting in homicide and suicide. Columbine, among others, will forever stand as a reminder of a tragic loss due to an act of vengeance.

Other Factors. These can range from accidental death by a discharged firearm to teens who kill for the thrill of it.

1.4B RESPONSES TO TEENAGE HOMICIDES
When teenagers die at the hands of another, the responses of those remaining can include—

- Shock and confusion regarding the senselessness of the act
- Guilt and blame, believing this act could have been prevented
- Fear of being victimized
- Anger, vengeance, and retaliation as a way to remedy the situation

1.4C TEENAGE SUICIDES
Teenage suicide is just as shocking and senseless as teen homicide. While more teenage girls *attempt* suicide, more teenage guys suc-

cessfully complete their suicide attempts. Adolescent guys tend to use suicidal means that are more violent and have less room for corrective measures.

Many times teen suicide follows a recognizable pathology, starting with teenage depression and alienation. This particular issue is covered more thoroughly in *What Do I Do When Teenagers Are Depressed and Contemplate Suicide?*, another book in this series. But for our purposes in this book, there are some important things a youth worker must understand when a teenager commits suicide.

First, a teen's death by suicide often leaves those left behind with a great sense of guilt. Family members and friends go through the mental anguish of thinking they could have—or should have—been the one to prevent this tragedy. They reconstruct the forensics of the teen's life and attempt to find the signs and reasons. They can become plagued with guilt over what they did or didn't do when warning signs were evidenced. This takes time and maybe even professional help to work through. Families also deal with shame when their teenager commits suicide, sometimes causing the family to withdraw from any outside support in a desire to keep the issue secret.

The second thing youth workers and parents must be aware of is the phenomenon of cluster suicides that could take place following the suicidal death of a teenager. Cluster suicides are a sudden epidemic of suicide attempts or deaths after the suicide of another teen. This can be brought on either by a tremendous feeling of loss or guilt over the friend's death or a newfound courage in those who've only contemplated suicide in the past but now feel emboldened to follow the example of the deceased teen. When a teenager dies, a lot of extra attention is focused on the situation.

This can cause other depressed teens to romanticize death, believing people will love and miss them more once they're gone. This postmortem popularity factor also plays into the phenomenon of cluster suicides. Youth workers and parents need to go on alert, keeping a watchful eye on sad, depressed and emotional teens after the suicide of another teenager in the community. And this is why it's so important to immediately bring counselors into youth groups and communities to help address the issue of a teen's suicide.

1.5 STAGES OF GRIEF

Death creates a state of bereavement and grief for many people. Bereavement means to be made desolate or totally deprived by death. Family members are often said to be bereaved after a loved one dies. Grief is the intense sorrow and mental anguish that's experienced through a loss. While grief can be the emotional expression that accompanies disappointment or misfortune, the grief of the bereaved is intense sorrow with suffering.

Experts who study grief have noticed certain patterns or elements that comprise the grieving process. Often they're labeled "stages of grief" because their normal pattern is successive; but in all honesty, all people grieve differently. When we talk about grieving adolescents, there are a number of additional factors we must understand. A teenager's cognitive ability and maturity aren't the same as adults'. Therefore, it's important to take into consideration the effects of the developmental process as it relates to adolescent grief.

Early adolescents may have a difficult time with the abstract concepts surrounding death. They understand the finality of it, but they may not be able to project the implications of loss as it affects the family. As a result, their grieving may be different from grown-ups'.

- Teens may feel sad and then, minutes later, be caught up in the thrill of a video game.
- Teens may exhibit a delayed reaction or seem affectless.
- Teens may be reluctant to talk about it because they don't have the cognitive ability to label what they feel or think.
- Teens may be more fearful after a loss, even fearing for their own safety. ("Who's going to take care of me?" "Are my friends going to die?" "Am I going to die?") Younger teens don't have the autonomy skills older teens do, so a fear of the loss of caregivers can be greater than the actual grief over a death.
- Teens' minds compartmentalize death in a more concrete way, so they may not understand the typical Christian phrases about death, such as "asleep in Christ," "passed on," or "went home to be with the Lord."
- Teens may make comments or ask questions that seem inappropriate, evidencing an immaturity in the way they cope with traumatic situations.

Middle and late adolescents have the cognitive ability to grasp the universality and inevitability of death. They come face-to-face with their own mortality when a peer dies. This is a sobering revelation for many older teens. Yet their immaturity shows the idealism of adolescence.

- They may contemplate suicide as a way of getting relief from their pain and a viable solution in the idealistic light of being with the departed friend or loved one.
- They may contemplate their regret over things said or not said, done or not done. This can also give rise to guilt.
- They may feel a sense of powerlessness played out in ideations that they could have prevented this or that things would have been so much better if *they* had died instead of their friend or loved one.
- As an act of defiance, they may consciously behave inappropriately so they don't have to face the pain of loss, deal with the reality, or think about the impending implications of death.

• They have the ability to engage the spiritual and theological aspects of death. This may lead them to question, doubt, or feel deceived by what they believe.

Youth workers must dispel ideas of normality: Grief is complex and how it manifests itself will vary from person to person. Some teens may not feel as intensely as others do. Therefore, they might believe they should grieve more. They might ask if it's wrong to have fun or why they don't feel anything. They may wonder how they "should" behave. They may not understand that grief can come in waves or cycles.

It's important to note that as youth workers deal with the grief of teenagers, they must understand that teens deal with grief at their own pace and in their own way. But if we're going to effectively help teens, then we must take into account *all* the following:

The Individual Teen. The relationship you have with a teenager will help you discern a sense of normalcy regarding the grief. You know the patterns and personality of the individual. Your gut response can help you gauge whether the teen is in danger.

The Stage of Adolescent Development. Knowing about teenagers' cognitive abilities, along with their emotional maturity, will help you discern their condition.

The Patterns or Stages of Grief. We'll explore these in the next section.

Common Behaviors. Youth workers must have a proper understanding of some of the behaviors common among adolescents in deep grief and bereavement. This includes recognizing the warning signs and symptoms that may indicate a grieving teen is at risk.

1.5A CLASSICAL STAGES OR PATTERNS OF GRIEF

The most foundational and groundbreaking studies on grief patterns came from Dr. Elisabeth Kübler-Ross. She worked all her life with dying patients and their grieving families. Her book *On Death and Dying* became the primer for our understanding of grief work.[13] Dr. Kübler-Ross recognized there are five stages to grief.[14] While it's difficult to witness stages in teens, these become more or less patterns teenagers slip in and out of, with mild to aggressive responses and with little to full resolve. I've added my own descriptions to Kübler-Ross' five stages.

Shock or Denial. This stage is very pronounced in teens because they experience not only the shock of the incident or news of their terminal illness, but also the shock of their own mortality. For many teens this may be the first time they've confronted death up close. They may say things like, "I can't believe this is happening," "I just saw that person yesterday," or "Teenagers don't die." They may expect the dead person to walk into the room at any moment, or they may talk as though this were a nightmare they hope to wake up from. Many times the trauma and shock are more emotional than the actual grief of loss. This stage is also accompanied by feelings of numbness and disbelief.

Anger. This is when a teenager actually starts to feel grief. Teens learn to mask their sadness with anger. Teenage guys will evidence this more than girls will because they don't want to be perceived as less than masculine—even in the face of death. They may be angry with the deceased for dying, with everyone else for asking them how they're feeling (this is misdirected anger and youth workers often get the brunt of this—don't take it personally), and with God for allowing this to happen.

Bargaining. This stage plays out more in the processing of a teen who's confronted by terminal illness. He may bargain with God for his own life or for the healing of a loved one. Or she may bargain for more time, pleading with God to let her or another person live to see another birthday or graduation. This pattern is evidenced in teens who face the traumatic death of a loved one through comments like, "I should have died instead of my friend" or, "If only I had done more." Guilt and regret may fill the pattern of bargaining in this instance. And when the bargaining doesn't pan out, teens may revert back to more pronounced forms of anger. Adolescents tend to be more physical in their emotional expressions. So if anger is rekindled, be aware it may play itself out in harmful ways (e.g., cutting, drug and alcohol use).

Depression. This pattern can play itself out in uncontrollable bouts of weeping to times of immobility, in which teens believe they can't overcome the sadness. Symptoms of depression (lack of concentration, changes in sleeping and eating patterns, feelings of dread and darkness, apathy) are pronounced in this stage of grief.

Acceptance. This is the point at which there is resolve. The terminally ill teen comes to terms with his own death or the imminent death of a loved one who's terminal. He may begin making arrangements for a funeral, writing a will, getting his affairs in order, and so on. When the friend or loved one of a teen dies tragically and unexpectedly, this stage looks more like the teen coming to an understanding that life continues. She may struggle to figure out how to adjust without the deceased. She may also express fears she'll forget the deceased.

1.5B COMMON BEHAVIORS AND RESPONSES OF ADOLESCENT GRIEF

Adolescents who are in the throes of grief may exhibit some of the following behaviors and responses:

- Teens may endure physical sickness—nausea, vomiting, head-aches, and stomachaches.
- Grief is exhausting, so teens may feel fatigued and lethargic.
- Teens may feel the need to remain strong and take care of others. When a friend dies, a teen may exhibit this behavior at home as well, caring for parents and siblings or—from a parent's perspective—becoming more responsible.
- Teens may find it difficult to concentrate because their conversations and thoughts are centered on the tragedy and the deceased.
- If a friend dies, teens may feel the need to confide in and be near their other friends, rather than adults. On the other hand, they may become clingy toward the surviving parent or another significant grown-up if a parent or adult loved one dies.
- Teens may have trouble completing tasks and doing school-work or their performance may be impaired.
- Teens may have nightmares that replay the trauma of a violent death.
- Teens may have radical mood swings—even more so than what's normal for adolescence. Common feelings include, but aren't limited to, anxiety, sadness, hurt, anger, rage, loneliness, confusion, isolation, guilt, regret, fear, panic, shock, fatigue, irritability, and being overwhelmed.
- Teens may feel a sense of entitlement, reprieve from daily responsibilities, or have an apathetic attitude because of the way they process the finality of death.
- Teens may withdraw or feel the need to be alone.
- Teens may feel the pain of other personal issues more acutely. (In other words, not having a prom date, not getting the part in the play or making the team, or feeling abandoned by their parents, will feel much worse to them than it normally would.)

This is sort of an avalanche effect in which the corollary pain others feel, along with the existing pain in the teen's life, is all lumped together into a greater grief.

- Teens may exhibit changes in sleeping and eating patterns for a brief period of time.
- Teens may idealize their relationship with the deceased and become critical of the family's decisions regarding everything from the funeral to acts of closure (decisions about the deceased's possessions).
- Teens may experience strong sensory recall, believing they heard or saw the deceased person. They may fear it's a ghost or the spirit of the dead. This can often follow an experience in which they encounter a voicemail, text message, or email left by the deceased. These are brain-fabricated illusions, suggestions, or memories that appear real to a vulnerable, grief-stricken teen.
- Teens may question and challenge their faith, beliefs, and theology. They may doubt the authenticity and validity of their faith and others'.

1.5C WARNING SIGNS AND SYMPTOMS OF ADOLESCENT GRIEF

Some teens have a difficult time coping with pain and suffering. They may begin to show some warning signs that they need help developing healthy coping skills. While pain and sorrow are natural when a person experiences the death of a friend or loved one, they become reminders and heighten the frustration of a teen who has poor coping skills to begin with.

Youth workers, parents, and teachers should mobilize resources and get help for teenagers who exhibit these warning signs and symptoms:

- Thoughts of suicide to stop the pain
- Cutting or other forms of self-injury and mutilation to dull the emotional pain by heightening the physical pain

- Alcohol or drug use or binging to escape the reality and ramifications of the death of a friend or loved one and numb the pain
- Increased anger that evidences itself in violent or hostile behavior such as vandalism, fighting
- Oppositional behaviors and defiance
- Engaging in promiscuous sexual activity in an attempt to eliminate the pain with hedonistic pleasure or fill the desires for closeness that were created in the void of their loss
- Increase in risk-taking and death-defying behaviors
- Disregard for responsibility, including truancy, academic failure, and withdrawal from school, work, and social activities
- Withdrawal, isolation, and avoidance of friends and family
- An obsession with death (i.e., hanging out in cemeteries, talking and writing about death, creating artistic depictions of death)
- Separation anxiety and increased phobias
- The surfacing of other mental health issues, such as eating disorders, conduct disorders, night terror disorder, abuse, addictions, and depression

If the above warning signs persist for two months after the death of a friend or loved one, or if they become more intense, then the adolescent should see a mental health professional immediately.

1.5D COMPLICATED GRIEF

As adolescents work through the normal process of grieving, they'll find that the strong feelings of sadness, hopelessness, and loss begin to diminish. The healthy grief process gradually moves from despair to resolve and life readjustment. But for a person experiencing complicated grief, this healthy process is damaged. They experience prolonged pain and suffering with an inability to cope or resume life. Complicated grief is a rare phenomenon, but it can affect some teens. When adolescents experience complicated grief, the first line of action is to get them professional help from a clinical therapist and medical treatment from a qualified psychiatrist. Treatment involves intensive counseling and may involve antidepressants and selective serotonin reuptake inhibitors (SSRIs).

Some of the signs of complicated grief include—

- Prolonged intense sorrow (four or more months) with no resolve or gradual decline in the pain and suffering
- Difficulty accepting the death of the loved one or friend, which may include an obsession with the deceased or constant pining for that person
- Emotional outbursts triggered by minor incidents or casual comments
- Symptoms similar to post-traumatic stress disorder, including unwarranted or uncontrolled thoughts, survivor guilt, sensitivity to any emotional stimuli, extreme agitation, and becoming easily startled or frightened
- A continued preoccupation with death and sorrow
- A sense of debilitation and immobility to perform even routine daily functions like hygienic care, getting dressed
- The absence of any type of pleasure and the inability to find joy in anything (anhedonia)
- They may end up withdrawing from people and then feel irritated when others try to help them. (People become an intrusion to a person with complicated grief.) As this progresses, the teen may even come to mistrust everyone.
- Inability to find meaning and significance in life apart from the deceased
- They may avoid anything that reminds them of the deceased for fear of experiencing an emotional outburst, including music, foods, people, places, activities, and so on.
- On the other hand, they may take on characteristics of the deceased, even believing they have symptoms of the same disease (if the deceased died of a terminal illness).
- Suicide ideation or attempts, including self-injury

In extreme cases the person may have delusional thoughts and conversations about the deceased. This may be evidenced in frequent comments such as, "When (name of the deceased) gets here…" or "I talked to (name of the deceased) on the phone today." And delusional behaviors may include leaving voice or text messages on the deceased's cell phone, sending him emails, and so on.

1.5E ANTICIPATORY GRIEF

Anticipatory grief is the normal mourning a teen and family may experience prior to death that's anticipated from a terminal illness. A teenager who has a terminal illness may experience this with his friends. A teenager may also feel this when a parent or loved one has a terminal illness. This form of grief has all of the natural signs and behaviors that occur in grief, but it happens prior to death and can be shared with the person who's dying.

This form of grief allows the teen to say good-bye, to get his affairs in order if he's dying, or to share his grief with the person who's terminally ill. Sometimes a teenager can't get beyond the denial and anger of a terminal illness. Grief is a process of "letting go," so anticipatory grief is a slow process of letting go prior to the person's death. Some teens may believe that to grieve before the friend or loved one dies is like abandoning the person—abandoning hope. If the teen remains in this state, then she hits the grieving stage of anger very hard. She may become extremely angry with the situation, God, and more so with herself. And the anger is often accompanied by great regret.

However, if a teen can come to terms with the death of a friend or loved one ahead of time, or with his own death, then it can offer many opportunities for healing, like being an active part in planning a funeral and saying good-bye to those who'll survive him or declaring his love for the one who's dying. And for the Christian, anticipatory grief can be a bittersweet time as talk turns toward eternity and the anticipation of reunion. This conversation is often reminiscent of someone who's about to take a trip knowing that the others will soon follow.

Even though grief work is done in light of anticipated death, we never fully resolve it until death finally occurs. Thus, while anticipatory grief can prepare the teenager for death, it cannot bring resolve until death actually occurs.

UNDERSTANDING HOW THEOLOGY INFORMS THE ISSUE OF DEATH

| SECTION 2 |

2.1 THEOLOGY OF DEATH

In the 23rd Psalm, David talks of walking through "the valley of the shadow of death" (NKJV). He speaks of the comfort of having a good Shepherd who walks with him and eliminates the fear of evil that may befall him. Many Christian teens interpret this passage to mean that facing death on its turf will be relatively painless and without suffering. Thus, they're often disillusioned when grief comes.

We learn a lot about death and how to respond to it from Jesus' example with Mary, Martha, and Lazarus in John 11. We see how Jesus is moved with compassion and weeps with Mary (John 11:35). Death brings sadness and suffering, but it also brings hope. Let's look at death from a theological perspective. (Note: This isn't a comprehensive theological approach, but it's intended to serve the purpose of helping teens.)

2.1A PHYSICAL DEATH IS INEVITABLE AND UNIVERSAL

In Genesis 2:17, God told Adam and Eve, "You must not eat from the tree of the knowledge of good and evil, for when you eat of it you will certainly die." So as a result of their disobedience to God, physical death entered the life cycle of humanity. This curse of death was passed to all living things, including plants and animals. Death resulted from sin, but God decided to redeem this problem. The tears, pain, and sorrow that accompany death are the parts we feel because of the curse of sin.

Ecclesiastes 3:1-2 reminds us there's a natural life cycle: "There is a time for everything, and a season for every activity under the heavens: a time to be born and a time to die, a time to plant and a time to uproot."

Psalm 39:4-5 and James 4:13-15 are passages that remind us of the brevity of life and the inevitability of death:

Show me, LORD, my life's end and the number of my days; let me know how fleeting my life is. You have made my days a mere hand-breadth; the span of my years is as nothing before you. Everyone is but a breath, even those who seem secure. (Psalm 39:4-5)

Now listen, you who say, "Today or tomorrow we will go to this or that city, spend a year there, carry on business and make money." Why, you do not even know what will happen tomorrow. What is your life? You are a mist that appears for a little while and then vanishes. Instead, you ought to say, "If it is the Lord's will, we will live and do this or that." (James 4:13-15)

In Psalm 89:48, the psalmist implies that no person can live without one day facing his own death: "Who can live and not see death, or who can escape the power of the grave?"

Romans 5:12 tells us death universally passes to all human-kind because of Adam's sin: "Therefore, just as sin entered the world through one man, and death through sin, and in this way death came to all people, because all sinned."

Hebrews 9:27-28 shows the inevitability of death in that it's appointed for each of us to die: "Just as people are destined to die once, and after that to face judgment, so Christ was sacrificed once to take away the sins of many; and he will appear a second time, not to bear sin, but to bring salvation to those who are waiting for him."

2.1B DEATH IS THE PASSAGEWAY INTO ETERNITY

Jesus tells Martha he's the resurrection and the life. Then he continues to say that even though a believer dies, that believer shall live eternally:

> Jesus said to her, "Your brother will rise again." Martha answered, "I know he will rise again in the resurrection at the last day." Jesus said to her, "I am the resurrection and the life. Anyone who believes in me will live, even though they die; and whoever lives by believing in me will never die. Do you believe this?" (John 11:23-26)

Paul indicates that when a believer is "away from the body" (dead) that believer is present with the Lord: "We are confident, I say, and would prefer to be away from the body and at home with the Lord" (2 Corinthians 5:8).

> Brothers and sisters, we do not want you to be uninformed about those who sleep in death, so that you do not grieve like the rest, who have no hope. We believe that Jesus died and rose again, and so we believe that God will bring with Jesus those who have fallen asleep in him. According to the Lord's word, we tell you that we who are still alive, who are left till the coming of the

Lord, will certainly not precede those who have fallen asleep. For the Lord himself will come down from heaven, with a loud command, with the voice of the archangel and with the trumpet call of God, and the dead in Christ will rise first. After that, we who are still alive and are left will be caught up together with them in the clouds to meet the Lord in the air. And so we will be with the Lord forever. Therefore encourage one another with these words. (1 Thessalonians 4:13-18)

Here Paul refers to Christians who've died as being "asleep" and waiting to be resurrected for eternity. He doesn't want the Thessalonians to be ignorant about this issue, explaining that all believers will be resurrected. For the believer, resurrection comes because Christ conquered death and was resurrected. The body appears to be asleep, but the soul and spirit are with the Lord.

First Corinthians 15:35-58 tells us resurrection isn't possible unless it's preceded by death. Jesus shares this analogy:

But someone will ask, "How are the dead raised? With what kind of body will they come?" How foolish! What you sow does not come to life unless it dies. When you sow, you do not plant the body that will be, but just a seed, perhaps of wheat or of something else. But God gives it a body as he has determined, and to each kind of seed he gives its own body. All flesh is not the same: Human beings have one kind of flesh, animals have another, birds another and fish another. There are also heavenly bodies and there are earthly bodies; but the splendor of the heavenly bodies is one kind, and the splendor of the earthly bodies is another. The sun has one kind of splendor, the moon another and the stars another; and star differs from star in splendor. So will it be with the resurrection of the dead. The body that is sown is perishable, it is raised imperishable; it is sown in dishonor, it is raised in glory; it is sown in weakness, it is raised in power; it is sown a natural body, it is raised a spiritual body. If there is a natural body, there is also a spiritual body. (vv. 15:35-44)

In Luke 16:19-31, Jesus tells a story about a rich man and a man named Lazarus. Both die and both are immediately in an eternal state:

"The time came when the beggar died and the angels carried him to Abraham's side. The rich man also died and was buried. In Hades, where he was in torment, he looked up and saw Abraham far away, with Lazarus by his side. So he called to him, 'Father Abraham, have pity on me and send Lazarus to dip the tip of his finger in water and cool my tongue, because I am in agony in this fire.' "But Abraham replied, 'Son, remember that in your lifetime you received your good things, while Lazarus received bad things, but now he is comforted here and you are in agony. And besides all this, between us and you a great chasm has been set in place, so that those who want to go from here to you cannot, nor can anyone cross over from there to us'" (vv. 22-26).

2.1C DEATH IS AN EVENT TO BUILD THE FAITH OF THOSE WHO GRIEVE

In John 11, Jesus was with his disciples when a message from Martha and Mary arrived, saying their brother, Lazarus, was extremely ill. The sisters implored Jesus to come and heal their brother. Jesus had a strong connection to this family, and he loved them very much. But still he waited until Lazarus died before announcing to the disciples it was time to go see Mary and Martha. In John 11:15, Jesus indicated that the faith of the disciples would be strengthened by this event. Later, in verse 26, Jesus asked Martha if she believed he's the resurrection, and she said she did believe.

We also see Mary and Martha grieving with many of their friends. When Jesus saw this, he grieved with them. Grief doesn't indicate a lack of faith. When the people were in the midst of their sorrow over Lazarus' death, God demonstrated his power and brought Lazarus back to life.

Job also realized this. In the midst of his overwhelming grief, Job proclaimed, "I know that my redeemer lives, and that in the end he will stand on the earth. And after my skin has been destroyed, yet in my flesh I will see God" (Job 19:25-26). Even in a time of incredible tragedy, Job's faith was strengthened.

The pain and suffering that came into the lives of these saints made them rely on God as their resurrection and Redeemer. Therefore, death and suffering can put us in a place to be more dependent on God and aware of God's work all around us.

2.1D DEATH IS AN OPPORTUNITY TO UNDERSTAND AND SHARE IN CHRIST'S SUFFERING

The prophet Isaiah told us the Messiah would be a "Man of sorrows" and "acquainted with grief" (Isaiah 53:3, NKJV). When we pray to be like Christ, do we expect we'll only join in his ministry of wise words and acts of kindness? Do we expect we'll only experience Jesus' power and presence? During his time on earth, Jesus was the Man of sorrows. He suffered and experienced great pain, sadness, and grief. Therefore, he understands what we feel, and he empathizes with us, giving us grace and mercy when we need it most:

> Therefore, since we have a great high priest who has ascended into heaven, Jesus the Son of God, let us hold firmly to the faith we profess. For we do not have a high priest who is unable to empathize with our weaknesses, but we have one who has been tempted in every way, just as we are—yet he did not sin. Let us

then approach God's throne of grace with confidence, so that we may receive mercy and find grace to help us in our time of need. (Hebrews 4:14-16)

But we can also become more like Jesus as we experience suffering. Jesus has a suffering love for a dying world. So as we experience someone's death, our grief and sadness give us a small perspective of so great a grief. And when we share our sorrow in light of Jesus' great sorrow, we come to understand the immense greatness of the joy that follows our grief.

2.1E TWO WAYS TO APPROACH DEATH

There are two helpful ways that we can face grief in death. The first is with hope, and the second is with comfort. Christians take solace in God's comfort and the hope of eternal life. Yet, unbelievers can also experience the comfort of God. This may be a good reminder in planning the funeral service for a believer and an unbeliever. Comfort is given to all out of the grace and compassion of God. But hope comes to the believer who knows and rests in the power of resurrection.

First, we'll look at hope.

"Brothers and sisters, we do not want you to be uninformed about those who sleep in death, so that you do not grieve like the rest, who have no hope" (1 Thessalonians 4:13). Paul is saying believers don't grieve like those who have no hope. Instead, the person who believes Jesus died and rose again lives in the hope of eternal life and the hope of being reunited with other believers in heaven someday.

"Do not let your hearts be troubled. Trust in God; trust also in me. My Father's house has plenty of room; if that were not so, would I have told you that I am going there to prepare a place for you? And if I go and prepare a place for you, I will come back and take you to be with me that you also may be where I am" (John 14:1-3). Jesus challenges us not to be heavy-hearted regarding death and the afterlife. The hope Jesus gives here is in the knowledge that he goes to prepare a place in heaven for those who are believers.

"Therefore my heart is glad and my tongue rejoices; my body also will rest secure, because you will not abandon me to the realm of the dead, nor will you let your faithful one see decay. You make known to me the path of life; you will fill me with joy in your presence, with eternal pleasures at your right hand" (Psalm 16:9-11). The author speaks of his secure rest in knowing that God doesn't abandon him in death. This knowledge breeds hope that leads to the joy of God's presence and eternal pleasures.

We're reminded death comes through the disobedience and sin of Adam, but our hope is that eternal life comes through the righteousness of Christ. Jesus has secured for us life in death:

For if, by the trespass of the one man, death reigned through that one man, how much more will those who receive God's abundant provision of grace and of the gift of righteousness reign in life through the one man, Jesus Christ! Consequently, just as one trespass resulted in condemnation for all people, so also one righteous act resulted in justification and life for all. For just as through the disobedience of the one man the many were made sinners, so also through the obedience of the one man the many will be made righteous. (Romans 5:17-19)

"When I saw him, I fell at his feet as though dead. Then he placed his right hand on me and said: 'Do not be afraid. I am the First and the Last. I am the Living One; I was dead, and now look, I am alive for ever and ever! And I hold the keys of death and Hades'" (Revelation 1:17-18). Jesus says he was dead but is now alive forevermore and has authority over death, reminding us once again of the hope we have in eternity.

Second, we'll look at God's comfort.

"You turned my wailing into dancing; you removed my sackcloth and clothed me with joy" (Psalm 30:11). Comfort came to the grieving psalmist when he saw God turn his grief into gladness.

"Even though I walk through the darkest valley, I will fear no evil, for you are with me; your rod and your staff, they comfort me" (Psalm 23:4). The shepherd's rod and staff become a source of comfort when people walk through death. These aren't tools of discipline. (If they were, what comfort would we find in them?) The rod and staff in the hands of the Shepherd bring comfort because they're weapons to fight off evil. He uses them to protect us when we're grieving.

The Messiah came to give comfort to all who mourn:

The Spirit of the Sovereign LORD is on me, because the LORD has anointed me to proclaim good news to the poor. He has sent me to bind up the brokenhearted, to proclaim freedom for the captives and release from darkness for the prisoners, to proclaim the year of the LORD's favor and the day of vengeance of our God, to comfort all who mourn, and provide for those who grieve in Zion—to bestow on them a crown of beauty instead of ashes, the oil of joy instead of mourning, and a garment of praise instead of a spirit of despair. They will be called mighty oaks, a planting of the LORD for the display of his splendor. (Isaiah 61:1-3)

We have a merciful Father in heaven who's the source of all comfort, and God gives us that comfort when we experience suffering:

> Praise be to the God and Father of our Lord Jesus Christ, the Father of compassion and the God of all comfort, who comforts us in all our troubles, so that we can comfort those in any trouble with the comfort we ourselves receive from God. For just as we share abundantly in the sufferings of Christ, so also our comfort abounds through Christ. If we are distressed, it is for your comfort and salvation; if we are comforted, it is for your comfort, which produces in you patient endurance of the same sufferings we suffer. And our hope for you is firm, because we know that just as you share in our sufferings, so also you share in our comfort. (2 Corinthians 1:3-7)

2.2 QUESTIONS THAT DEMAND THEOLOGICAL CONSIDERATION

When someone close to us dies, it can create a theological dilemma for us. The answers that were so cut-and-dried in our minds now seem hollow and nonsensical in reality of death's darkness. Death may cause us to rethink our theology or make us wrestle though theological paradigms and how they inform real-life situations.

In the following paragraphs, I've detailed some of the major questions people face when they confront death. There really aren't any concrete answers for them. Volumes have been written on each question, so you won't find comprehensive answers here. I've merely provided this list to help you better prepare as you help grieving teens and families search out answers. I believe it's important for youth workers and parents to acknowledge that while they may not have the answers to these questions, they still must commit to lovingly walk with students and their families through the pain.

This journey is part of what makes us a community of faith.

2.2A WHY DOES GOD ALLOW TRAGEDY, DEATH, AND SUFFERING?

At the heart of this question is the limited understanding of an unlimited God, as well as the clash of some basic doctrine—like the sovereignty of God, the question of evil, God's love and goodness, and the injustice of pain and suffering.

We get a greater understanding of God's role in pain and suffering when we live into the hope that God continuously and eternally redeems us and the world. God makes all things right. Yet, while this is true, it doesn't satisfy the present suffering faced by grieving teens and families.

Jesus said, "[God] causes his sun to rise on the evil and the good, and sends rain on the righteous and the unrighteous" (Matthew 5:45). It doesn't seem fair when we're in the middle of suffering, yet we see wicked people prospering. Christians hold on to the fact that suffering is only for a season because of the hope we have in a redeeming, resurrected Savior.

Redemption and reconciliation aren't a single act but a continuous event. God is always redeeming us and our situations— moment by moment. This is why we can begin to look in a forward direction and believe by faith that "in all things God works for the good of those who love him, who have been called according to his purpose" (Romans 8:28).

A day will come when God will eliminate pain, suffering, and death. And on that day God will wipe away every tear from our eyes. Revelation 21:3-5 says—

> And I heard a loud voice from the throne saying, "Now the dwelling of God is with men, and he will live with them. They will be his people, and God himself will be with them and be their God. He will wipe every tear from their eyes. There will be no more death or mourning or crying or pain, for the old order of things has passed away." He who was seated on the throne said, "I am making everything new!" Then he said, "Write this down, for these words are trustworthy and true." (NIV)

2.2B IS THE DEAD PERSON IN HEAVEN?

Christian teens or their family members will often ask this question when they're in the throes of grief over a deceased non-Christian loved one (or a loved one with unknown beliefs). When presented with this question, it's probably not a good time to offer a lesson on the eternal state of those who die. Something to consider before you answer: "The LORD does not look at the things human beings look at. People look at the outward appearance, but the LORD looks at the heart" (1 Samuel 16:7).

Through the centuries the church has held to a strong view that salvation comes through Christ alone, but it's been debated as to when the salvific process ceases. Some believe Christ's love and salvation are made clear to the individual before death, and then death becomes the final barrier to that offer of salvation. Others believe that Christ meets the individual at death and offers salvation. And still others believe death isn't a barrier for the eternal love and atonement of Christ, meaning Christ's love is extended to a person even beyond death.

Now I know these views may be making your head spin—good! That means you have some homework to do. There are many books on the eternal state of the lost and the process of salvation. Start researching and reading. But be aware a grieving heart will seek answers.

For the Christian, Paul says, "We are confident, yes, well pleased rather to be absent from the body and to be present with the Lord" (2 Corinthians 5:8, NKJV).

2.2C SHOULD WE REMOVE LIFE SUPPORT?

Youth workers may find themselves in the middle of an ethical and theological discussion when parents face the decision of whether to take their teenager off life support. Medical technology, while good, has generated some ethical and theological dilemmas that aren't directly addressed in Scripture. Because of modern medical technology, the body can be kept alive (breathing and blood circulating) through the use of advanced life-support systems. The controversy comes in determining the point of death. And the issue becomes even more complex with the possibility of an organ transplant, whereby the body can be kept alive until the organs are harvested.

This ethical debate gave rise to the Uniform Determination of Death Act (U.D.D.A.), which defines the death of an individual as, "An individual who has sustained either: (1) irreversible cessation of circulatory and respiratory functions, or (2) irreversible cessation of all functions of the entire brain, including brain stem, is dead. A determination of death must be made in accordance with accepted medical standards."[15] Therefore, if the brain ceases to function, then the person can be deemed "brain dead" or clinically dead. The U.D.D.A. served to determine the legal death of a person, as well as the medical definition of the death of a person. At least 31 states have adopted this statement to define death.

When parents are in the midst of making the decision to cease life support, they're rarely concerned with the ramifications of a euthanasia controversy. They need assurance there's no possibility of recovery. Given that, they need further assurance that they're giving their child a great gift by releasing him from the bondage of these life-support machines and into the care and presence of God. They're also giving others a great gift of life by allowing the donation of viable organs.

2.2D IS CREMATION BIBLICALLY ACCEPTABLE?

Questions may arise regarding the sanctity of cremation. Does the Bible speak against such practices? If the body is the temple of the Holy Spirit and if there's to be a bodily resurrection, is cremation a disrespectful process? The Bible doesn't speak directly to the issue of cremation, and it gives no evidence that such a funeral practice runs counter to biblical directives. Scripture does tell us we're made from the dust of the earth, and that we'll return to that state (Genesis 3:19).

Cremation is basically an expedited version of what will naturally occur over time. Some believe that burning the body is a dishonoring practice (based on Old Testament accounts where the body was burned because of sin issues; see Leviticus 20:14 and

Joshua 7:15). This was juxtaposed against countless passages that speak of burial as an acceptable or common practice. Most theologians, from the conservative to the liberal, have agreed that the cultural practice of the final disposition of the dead is not a moral issue addressed in Scripture.

Catholic tradition does not speak against cremation, but it gives some guidelines on how the process should be done. The instructions state that cremated remains are to be treated with the same dignity as the human body from which they've come. Burial should be the primary mode, since it follows Christ's example; but cremation is still permissible. Scattering ashes at sea, from the air, or on the ground, or keeping the remains in one's home are viewed as being an irreverent disposition for burial.[16]

2.3 SCRIPTURE PASSAGES TO CONSIDER

- 2 Samuel 12:15-23—David finds comfort as he mourns over the terminal illness and death of his child.
- 2 Samuel 18:33-19:4—David mourns the death of his son Absalom.
- Psalm 46:1-3—God is our Refuge in troubled times.
- Matthew 11:28—Jesus invites those who carry a heavy burden to find rest in him.
- Mark 5:22-23, 35-43—Jesus resurrects Jairus' 12-year-old daughter.
- Luke 7:11-15—Jesus engages the funeral of the teenage son of the widow of Nain and brings the young man back to life.
- 1 Corinthians 15:20-22—Christ, the firstfruits of the dead, makes many alive.
- 2 Corinthians 5:1-6—Paul speaks of the frailty and limits of the physical body in light of a resurrected and glorified body.

PRACTICAL ACTION TO TAKE WHEN DEATH AFFECTS A YOUTH GROUP

| SECTION 3 |

3.1 PRACTICAL HELP FOR YOUTH WORKERS

Death is not a common occurrence on the landscape of youth ministry. Many professional youth workers go their entire careers without experiencing the death of a student. However, you may find yourself in a situation like Pastor Dave's at the beginning of this book, where you're called upon to be a point person during a crisis. Families may look to you for guidance or support. In this section I'll offer some suggestions as to what you can do or say during various scenarios when you're helping those who've encountered a death.

3.2 HELPING A FAMILY

Rarely do people plan for death, especially the death of a teenager. Unless death by terminal illness has been looming, families are often caught off guard. Families will usually seek assistance from their pastors during this difficult time, and hospitals will bring in chaplains for those families who don't have church connections. The pastor becomes a vital person in the care of a family during bereavement, whereas a teenager may need your assistance once death takes a family member or friend.

Grieving families are thrown into chaos. They're quickly overwhelmed by not only the death, but also all the activities and details that come after losing someone to death. A spiritual caregiver can serve to help the family navigate these troubled waters. When you get a call like Pastor Dave did, here are some things you should do:

3.2A IMMEDIATE RESPONSE

Be Available. This is the first and primary response a youth worker should engage. Go immediately to be with the grieving family or the teen who's lost a family member. A family in grief needs to have a point person helping them. If there are close extended family members nearby, one of them may serve as the point person for the family, making calls to notify other family members, schools, employers, coaches, and so on, and caring for the family's day-to-day needs. In this case, you may serve as a liaison between your church and the grieving family, a typical role for a youth worker when death invades a youth group. However, if no relative is available to serve as the family's point person, then you can offer your services and be available to the grieving family—daily.

Family Care. Families in grief are often thrown into the hectic schedule of frequenting hospitals, making arrangements for the deceased, filling out reams of paperwork, attempting to host out-of-town family members, and so on. So many times the routine daily tasks can be overlooked, including preparation of meals, childcare, and grocery shopping. Arranging to have these things done by members of your congregation can be a very powerful ministry to a grieving family.

Hospital Leadership. If you're called to the hospital, you may find that other church members, extended family, and many teenagers show up there. You can assist the family by organizing and managing these additional visitors.

- Keep people congregated in a separate area so the family can be protected. In this way you may serve as a kind of "bodyguard" to keep people out of the way.
- Organize a time of prayer in the hospital waiting room. It's often good to delegate this job to someone so you can be more available to the family.
- Communicate information between the family and the people who've come to support them.
- Start organizing extended care for the family by asking people to commit to bring meals. Provide a sheet of paper and literally sign people up. Their presence is an indication they're willing to help.

Funeral Preparation. A family may feel helpless, panicked, or overwhelmed when it comes to starting the funeral process. It's possible they've never done this before, so they may look to you for help. Assure the family they're not alone as they go through this difficult process. Many of the actual funeral arrangements can be made under the guidance of a funeral director.

The sequence will go as follows:

- At the point of death, the family must contact a mortuary or funeral home, usually one that's close to their home or that their church has worked with in the past.
- The family must sign a release form so the mortuary can pick up the body of the deceased. This must be done even if the hospital or coroner's office contacts the mortuary.

- The family should arrange to meet with the funeral director to discuss the details of the funeral. It's good for the youth worker or pastor (whoever will serve as the funeral officiant) to attend this meeting.
- Prior to this meeting, ask the family who they'd like to serve as the funeral officiant. Some families want clergy who are family members or longtime friends to officiate the ceremony; others may call on the youth worker to do this.

The officiant should work with the family to plan the funeral service or memorial and the final words at the interment (gravesite); help with the selection of pallbearers and the organization of a meal for family and friends after the ceremony; and advise the family as to where funds can be directed if people want to make memorial donations.

The funeral director will—

- Arrange to transport and prepare the body for viewing or cremation
- Make sure all legal documents, such as the death certificate, are secured
- Assist the family in the selection of a casket, outer burial container, urn, cemetery plot, headstone or grave marker, and so on
- Help establish visitation times, funeral and gravesite times, and other preparations (unless the family wants this done at the church, in which case the responsibility falls on the church leader to arrange the times and clear the church calendar)
- Help with obituary notices and printed visitation cards
- Be available for the visitation and funeral, organizing and coaching pallbearers and funeral processions
- Help arrange aftercare for a grieving family (if the church doesn't do this)

- Provide pricing for all services rendered by the funeral home and cemetery

Coordinating Church Support. Bad news travels fast, and information concerning the death of a student can spread through a church like wildfire. It's important you do some quick fact-finding and get the family's permission to share the news. Many times the family will be grateful you're doing this for them. It's also important you include directives in your messages to people, asking them to respect the privacy of the family and notifying them of ways they can help through the coordinated efforts of the church.

Here's a plan you can follow—

- Gather vital information that needs to be communicated: The name(s) of the student(s) who died; the cause of death; where it occurred; the visitation and funeral arrangements, if they've been made (if not, direct people to the church's Web site where those announcements will be posted); the state of the family; anything else the family wishes to communicate to people.
- Have a prepared statement that can be posted on a Web page or given to the media. A prepared statement helps protect the family—and you—from disclosing any information that's confidential or privy to only a few. Having the family sign off on the statement ahead of time e   nsures that their wishes and needs are respected.
- Be aware that when teenagers die tragically, the media often makes it newsworthy (sometimes at the expense of hurting people). You may have to run interference for a family by asking the media not to contact the family and not allowing the media to be present at funeral or visitation ceremonies. Coach all leadership and staff to avoid the media. Designate a spokesperson on behalf of the church and the grieving family to

deliver a prepared statement. Make sure everyone knows who that person is and directs all inquiries to that spokesperson.

- Directly notify church staff, members of leadership, and paid and volunteer youth ministry staff about the death first. If people are looking for information, chances are they'll contact those in leadership. Coach them as to what's being said (and what shouldn't be said) regarding the arrangements. Be aware information that shouldn't be disclosed includes the actions of others, the wishes and private dealings of the family, and any legal information or information that may involve a police investigation, and so on.

- Be prepared to make public announcements on behalf of the family. This would include telling the church family during a service and making students aware in the youth group.

- Be prepared to ask church members to assist in the care of the family. This ranges from telling them to be sensitive about contacting the family to helping with the funeral service.

- You may also want to organize meals for the family. The person who coordinates this should keep in mind any additional family members who may be staying with or visiting the grieving family. Meals don't need to be multiple courses, but they should be appropriate to accommodate any children present. A coordinator must tell people what to bring. This avoids the awkward embarrassment of making the family eat lasagna every night for two weeks. The coordinator should also be in contact with the family to arrange meal drop-off times, for special dietary needs, and so on. Restaurant gift cards are also a great gift to provide during hectic hospital stays.

- Designate someone to coordinate transportation and child care for the family, if needed. Child care can involve taking younger children to practices, games, or any other special activities they may be involved in. Other services can include pet care and laundry. (Having a sick teen at home can produce a lot of laundry.) These services may go on for a month or so.

- If there's a terminal illness that precedes the death, a church may serve the family well by coordinating these types of services throughout the months of the illness. (Remember, being deemed "terminal" marks about a six-month period.) Doing so will not only help a family with the hectic schedule of care, but also alleviate a bit of the family's financial strain.

- If the funeral will be at the church, clear church calendars quickly. Make sure the facility is prepared to accommodate many people from the community.

Listen. The family may want to talk, so you should be available to listen. This is a time when you may want to speak less and not be quick to advise. Often when you sit down to plan a funeral service, parents may begin to reminisce and become emotional. This is a part of the grieving and healing process. Allow them a lot of room to do that. You may also want to ask how family members are feeling. Ask each family member directly and privately. Realize that the chaos of planning a funeral and coming through the trauma of death hasn't allowed the family members time to process their own emotions. By asking them how they're feeling and allowing enough time for them to be heard, you give them an opportunity to break free from the details and to process their grief and pain. Be aware they may not want to do this or may not be ready to do it just yet. Be sensitive by not forcing the issue.

Assist with Difficult Tasks. A family may elicit your help and support in accomplishing a variety of tasks that are either part of the grieving process or your help to finalize their grieving. These tasks may be difficult for the youth worker as well, due to the emotions involved. Some may include—

- Addressing a sports team or small group the teenager was involved in
- Depending upon the time and circumstances of the death, parents may ask you to break the news to the teen's special

friends one-on-one. This may include the teen's best friend or a girlfriend or boyfriend.

- Helping parents clean out a bedroom, locker, or dorm room
- Participating in a private ritual ceremony such as the spreading of ashes
- Helping parents donate some of the teen's possessions
- If there is a traumatic or violent death, you may be asked (for a number of reasons) to accompany a family to court or even to testify. If this is difficult for you, be prepared to talk it through with a counselor.
- Accompanying the family on a visit to an accident site
- Addressing students at the deceased teen's school
- Revisiting sites where spiritual milestones occurred in the teen's life, such as camp, the place where the teen was baptized, and so on
- Helping parents sort through photos and read through personal journals and writings to compile or create a tribute Web page or book
- Provide support at a local high school for grieving students

If a parent dies and the teen was close to that parent, then you may be asked to occasionally fill that parental role. You may also be asked to accompany a teenager to the hospital when a parent is taken off life support.

Be Available after the Funeral. The days following a funeral tend to be very difficult for grieving family members. This is actually the time when they truly begin the grief process. The funeral is over, out-of-town guests and families have gone, and the steady stream of visitors has ended. And the death of a teen leaves a big void the family must now confront and live with.

A family will go through a readjustment period. Your continued involvement in the life of that family may be critical to their readjustment. Some ways a youth worker can assist the family through their grief and readjustment are—

- Remember to visit and call the family long after the trauma is over.
- Remember anniversary dates (the teen's birthday, death, holidays). These times are often difficult for a family, and your presence can be a huge ministry.
- If the family was active in the support of the youth ministry, keep them involved. For example, if they opened their home to students, ask them if you can still use their home.
- Encourage the teen's good friends to visit the family. The most tragic feeling a family will face is isolation.

3.2B HELPING A TERMINALLY ILL TEENAGER FACE DEATH

If you're particularly close to a teen who is terminally ill or his family, you may be involved in the process of helping that teenager face death. It's a slow and reserved process. First off, you must remain positive. Always talk of hope: Hope in the medical process, hope in the goodness of God, and even hope in death. Don't make promises on God's behalf, such as telling teens God will miraculously cure them. That may not be God's plan, but you can tell them with assurance that someday things will be amazing for them and their family.

Here are a few tips you can follow when dealing with a terminally ill teenager:

- Realize that the teen will go through the five stages of grief over her impending death: Shock or denial over the news, anger, bargaining with God, depression, and then acceptance. There is no timetable for this process, and it's more complicated for a dying teenager who must also battle the ravages of an illness in her body. Patiently listen to her.

- Realize the powerful ministry of presence. You may never know the comfort you bring by just being with the teen and his family. Sometimes there is nothing to say, nor are any words expected. Just be available!

- Let the teen talk about what she's going through. People may be afraid to give a dying person the opportunity to talk about death, for fear of creating a doomsday atmosphere. But dancing around the issue doesn't help a teen who desires to talk about it.

- Answer any questions to the best of your ability. You may find that a teenager facing death becomes profoundly spiritual, asking questions most people do not. He may want to know about heaven and hell; he may ask about meeting loved ones who've already died; he may speak of his desire to quickly encounter Christ. Always help the teen to see God's grace, love, and goodness.

- A teen may have concerns about the affairs she's leaving behind. She may want assurance that family members, especially younger siblings, will be attended to. She may have concerns about the care of a pet. You can encourage the teen to get her affairs in order. This means you can empower her and then walk alongside her as she takes care of some of these concerns herself. By doing this, you not only help the teen finalize some things, but also give her the needed autonomy and control that tends to be taken away from a teenage patient who faces death.

- There may be a time when the teen faces fear. A terminal illness and death can be very scary. We have to realize that the next and very imminent life event for this teen isn't the prom or graduation or college, but dying. Again, the best thing a youth worker can do is listen, validate what the teen feels, and feel it (empathize) with him.

- A teen may have the desire to do something prior to dying. This can range from attending a concert to traveling to an exotic place. Parents of terminal children, often by instinct, attempt to fulfill these wishes. And when those wishes are beyond the family's means, there are organizations such as the Make-A-Wish Foundation (www.wish.org) that help fulfill them. But a youth group can also help by doing small things like accommodating the teen's special needs to make sure she can be a part of an activity, even if it's only for a short time. Or they can throw a surprise party for the teen, even when it's not her birthday.

- Finally, you may be one of many people who need to give the teenager permission to die. It's very befitting to talk from your heart when you do this. Assure the teen that God will take care of everyone here. Let him know he's loved and he will be missed and not forgotten. Assure him of the hope of being reunited again.

3.2C WHAT'S IT GOING TO BE LIKE BEFORE DEATH COMES?

Many youth workers have never walked into a room where a person is moments away from dying. This can be a very traumatic experience. This section will serve as a practical template for what you might see and expect.

First, family members may be wrestling with the fact that death is finally approaching. This can be a peaceful, yet sorrowful, resolve for some family members. They may want time alone with the dying teen, although this is often impossible because other family members don't want to be absent when death arrives. You might hear family members say their last good-bye or give permission to the dying teen to go into the arms of Christ.

If you're allowed the privilege of sharing this moment with a family, it will be very emotional. You don't need to hide your emotions during this time. A common mistake is for a youth worker to believe he should be emotionless as a sign of strength. An emotionless response doesn't communicate strength, but it may communicate a lack of compassion. Compassion means you suffer with the family.

Also be sensitive to the fact that the family may not want anyone other than immediate family in the room. You should ask, "Would you like to be alone as a family now?" If the answer is affirmative, then lead by helping clear the room of everyone who's non-family. Tell the family you'll be outside until they call you. When the teen dies, most likely someone will come out and invite you back into the room.

Some family members, like younger siblings, may not be as resolved to see the teen die. You may want to stay close to those family members and minister to their needs while the rest of the family focuses their attention on the patient. Be ready for responses of anger or rage, a show of no emotion, or a sense of bitterness from those family members.

Before death arrives, the dying teen will be in the stage, or syndrome, of imminent death. This may last anywhere from 6 to 24 hours, and it has some concrete visible symptoms:

- The teen will be bedbound and may have lapses of cognitive coherence. This means she may or may not recognize people, and she may or may not be able to answer questions. She may be too weak to speak, but she can communicate with smiles, opening her eyes, or slight hand and head movements.
- The teen may exhibit hypoactive or hyperactive delirium, falling in and out of sleep for short periods of time.

- The teen may begin running a fever and experience a pooling of saliva, which causes a noise known as a "death rattle." This is due to the loss of the swallowing reflex. Many times an attending nurse or doctor will monitor this.
- In the final stages, the teen may slip into a coma. His extremities (hands and feet, arms and legs) may begin to grow cold, and his respiration may become more difficult or labored. This is known as dyspnea. This may evidence itself in louder short and shallow breaths to longer and less frequent labored breaths or occasional gasps of air.
- At some point a doctor may discuss a treatment plan and advance directive with the family.
- If there is no brain activity, ventilators may be turned off, treatment may cease altogether, or medications may be increased for the patient's comfort. This step will hit the family hard as the reality sinks in that the next event in their lives is the death of their teen.
- Doctors will continue to monitor the patient until a pronouncement of death is made. (This scenario may look different when the teen dies at home, as there are no monitors, ventilators, etc. But the teen's vital signs will be monitored under the care of an attending nurse or hospice caregiver.)
- The sounds of the teen's labored breathing will cease, indicating that the teen has died. Vital signs will be checked, and a pronouncement of death is made. The family may want time alone with the deceased teen at this point. If the teen is in a hospital room, the family is allowed to stay as long as they need.
- Then the body will be released to a morgue, and the funeral home, chosen by the family, will be notified. If the teen dies at home, the visiting nurse or hospice worker must contact the office of the deputy coroner, who will authorize the movement of the body, and the funeral home will be notified by the coroner's office.

In the event the teen is an organ donor, the family may never see the cessation of breathing or the ventilators powered down. Ventilators and machines can maintain the patient's respiration, circulation, body temperature, blood pressure, and fluids when a patient has nonviable brain function. If the teen is said to have a nonviable brain or, more commonly, determined to be brain dead, then a pronouncement of death is made by a physician. Time of death is chosen when a physician determines that the entire brain and brain stem has irreversibly lost all neurological function. However, life support may be kept active to keep all vital organs viable until they can be harvested for a recipient. Families are encouraged to say their last good-byes. And when the family is gone, the body is taken away.

You may walk into a hospital room where the teen has already been pronounced dead. This usually occurs when a teen has been tragically killed. You need to be prepared for what you may see.

- As I mentioned earlier, family grief at the loss of a child is overwhelming. Family members may have arrived shortly before you. They may wail in sorrow, exhibit hysterics, and even become physically ill or faint. This type of brokenness makes the largest of men and women seem frail and small, and rightfully so. They're experiencing a deep grief. Some family members may hold the body of their teen or have a difficult time letting it go.
- If the death was extremely tragic, the teen's body may be disfigured. This could include lacerations, bruises, broken bones, and swelling that could render the teen unrecognizable. Face and head wounds often occur in accidents, so the teen's head may be shaved and her face bandaged.
- Many times the teen will have been intubated. This means a breathing tube has been placed down her throat to help

her breathe. In addition, she may be hooked up to monitors, with numerous tubes and wires.

- At the time of death, the body becomes ashen in color, and the skin, feet, and hands may turn a purplish-blue. The body's temperature begins to lower, so the teen may be cold to the touch, depending on when death occurred.

This might be a good place for me to make this point: A friend (boyfriend or girlfriend) of the teen may be with you, or other friends may arrive on the scene. If they're allowed to see their friend in this state, you may need to prepare them by describing what they're about to see. Additionally, you may need to prepare students for what they'll see at a wake or funeral. Many teenagers have never been to a death ritual. Obviously, they won't see what you see in a hospital room, but they should be prepared nonetheless.

When a youth worker is with a family at the time of death, she may find it difficult to know what to say. Here are some tips:

- Express your condolences and personal sorrow to the family.
- Share a fond memory, story, or observation and verbalize your love for the deceased teen. Families often begin to experience healing by talking about the wonderful moments, character quirks, and humorous experiences they had with their child. You may experience moments of laughter in the midst of great sorrow. Point to this as evidence of the hope we have in Christ and that someday we'll be reunited to experience even greater joy.
- Acknowledge the difficulty of the situation by admitting that words may not adequately convey the depth of loss they're feeling. It isn't bad to admit it's difficult to know what to say in this situation.
- Express your support and the support of the church by proactively telling the family what the church will do for them. (In other words, prepare meals, help with funeral preparations,

run transportation to the airport to pick up out-of-town relatives and friends, arrange for child care, and so on.) Do this instead of saying, "If there's anything we can do..."
• Offer to pray for and with the family.

Then don't say anything—just be available to console, cry with, and love a family suffering.

3.2D PLANNING A FUNERAL, MEMORIAL, OR COMMITTAL SERVICE

A family may call upon the youth worker to officiate the funeral service of their teenager. Since many youth workers don't do this very often, I thought it would be wise to walk through some steps here. You need to know the difference between a funeral service, a memorial service, and a committal service.

But before I explain those three types of services, let's get a broader understanding of the sequence of death rites and rituals. That term sounds creepy, but it's an accurate description of the events that culminate in friends and family finally letting go of the deceased. Some families have strong ethnic backgrounds and may incorporate the ceremonies (or portions of them) from their heritage.

For example, some Jewish Christians have incorporated a practice called *shemira* into their death ritual. This is a practice of guarding or watching over the body of the deceased. As a way of honoring the dead person, from the point of death until the burial, someone stands watch and recites the Psalms. Thus, the body is never left alone until after the burial. You need to be aware practices and rituals like this one may be a part of the family's wishes for their departed.

More commonly in Western culture, the rituals may follow this order: After the family has made the funeral arrangements with the mortuary, they may decide to have a viewing of the body for friends and family members. This is sometimes called a visitation or more commonly known as a wake. Like the *shemira*, a wake came from the practice of watching guard or staying watchfully alert until the body was buried. Usually a wake can take place one or two evenings before the funeral. The mortuary arranges this, taking into account the amount of time needed to get a certificate of death and prepare the body.

There is no service during the wake. Friends and family come to the funeral home (or, depending on ethnic practice, the person's home) to see the body and give condolences to the grieving family. This practice brings closure to a lot of people. The body is in the casket and, based upon the wishes of the family, the casket may remain open until the end of the funeral service. If the body has been severely damaged during an accident, the family may elect to have a closed casket during the wake and funeral. Some families decide to do this even when the body is intact, so they can remember images from when the person was living, rather than dead. You can minister to a family during the days of the wake by caring for children or making sure they have food brought to them.

A funeral service usually takes place a day or two after the visitation or wake. Some families may elect not to have any visitation or wake and just do a funeral service. This is a ceremony that honors the dead. And for the Christian, it celebrates the hope of eternal life. This ceremony can be done in the funeral home, but many want to have the funeral service in a church. If so, the body is brought to the church by the mortician. It may be brought in as part of a ceremonial processional that's followed by the family, or more commonly it's situated in the front of the sanctuary with the casket open for all to view.

At the end of the ceremony, mourners are usually invited to pass by the casket one final time. The family remains until everyone has left. Then the funeral director closes the casket, and the pallbearers carry it to the hearse and it's taken to the gravesite. If you officiate the ceremony, you may need to know who the pallbearers are and direct them to the funeral director. Usually eight pallbearers are chosen from among those who had significant relationships with the deceased. Pallbearers aren't selected from the immediate family so as to honor their grief.

If you're asked to do the funeral of an adult (perhaps the parent of a student or youth volunteer), you may want to check with the funeral director and family members to see if there will be any military rituals in the ceremony. If a person served in the military, oftentimes the government (in many countries) will ceremonially present a flag to the family, commemorating the deceased's record of military service. This is often done through the mortuary and the flag is folded and placed in a display case near the coffin. If the deceased was active in the military at the time of death (I have known youth workers who were called upon to do the funerals of a late adolescent from their youth ministry who was killed in the line of duty) there may be an honor guard, military representative, or soldiers (pallbearers) in military dress present. If this is the case, military honors of presenting a flag to the family and an honor guard salute may become part of the ceremony.

Some families don't have a funeral service because they may have chosen to have the body cremated. In that event there's no hurry to have a funeral, so a memorial service is planned. This is done at the family's leisure and usually coordinates around the schedules of family members who may need to travel to attend the ceremony. Sometimes both a funeral and a memorial service are done, with the memorial service being held in a different location (city, state) to accommodate others.

A memorial service celebrates the life of the deceased. It's similar to the funeral service, and many elements of the service can be interchanged. One noticeable difference is that the funeral service tends to be more solemn because it's very close to the time of death. A memorial service allows some distance and leaves some room for grieving in between the death and the actual service. As a result this type of service tends to be less solemn. In the event a teenager dies, a family may elect to have a closed funeral with only family and a few close friends in attendance. Then a couple of weeks later, they'll have a memorial service friends can attend.

A committal service is a very short service that takes place at a gravesite, cemetery mausoleum, or a place where the ashes will be scattered. This is usually a very short service involving the reading of a Scripture passage, a few brief remarks, and then a closing prayer. Afterward, the funeral director may comment on this being the end of the ceremony and will usually direct people back to their cars. Committal services can involve family members dropping dirt or laying flowers onto the casket as they leave. Many times people will return to the church or a hall where they can have a meal with the family.

If you're called upon to help plan a funeral service, you'll need to sit with the family and find out what some of their wishes are for this service. When a teenager dies of a terminal illness, it's likely that the student had some wishes for her funeral. Some students write notes or poems to be read, or request certain songs to be played. These should be included in the service. If the service is for a deceased parent or loved one, it's often a very healing gesture to involve the grieving teenager in the planning of the funeral or memorial.

There are a few additional elements that should be included in a funeral or memorial service:

Music. For the Christian, worship becomes a part of the celebration of a funeral. Include the student's favorite worship songs. It's also very appropriate to have someone sing or play music as a special part of the service. This element may be difficult to organize if the funeral is held during the day, because it may require musicians, who may not know the deceased, to take time off work.

Scripture Reading. In section 2 of this book, I've listed a number of passages that may be used during a funeral service. It's important to note here that while there is sorrow surrounding death, Christians sorrow with the hope of someday being united with loved ones and Christ. I also make it a point to remind people the hope we have rests in the joy of knowing that the deceased is more alive and healthy than those who were left behind. In the event the deceased was not a Christian or you don't know the life of the person, it's better to focus on the comfort God brings to those who feel sorrow. He redeems all situations. Be sensitive and understand that a funeral or memorial service is not a revival or evangelistic meeting.

Homily. This is a very short devotional or commentary on the Scripture passage. It's usually done by the officiant.

Eulogy. The family may ask you or others to give a eulogy. Typically the officiant gives a eulogy, but it's not uncommon to have other close relatives or friends share as well. A eulogy is a tribute to the deceased. It can include facts like the full name of the deceased, the dates of birth and death, names of the survivors (parents and siblings' full names), details about work, school, home, achievements, stories, and memories. A eulogy should be about three to five minutes long.

IMPORTANT NOTE

It's never a good idea to have an open microphone at the funeral or memorial service of a teenager. This is an emotional time for students, even students who may not have known the deceased very well. From my experience, the funeral of a teen is a packed event and well attended by teenagers. An open microphone can become an opportunity for hurting, attention-seeking kids to grandstand. In addition, it can create an avalanche effect in which every student believes he or she should say something. This quickly becomes awkward because it's difficult to control, especially if teens are sharing their grief. And then if an adult intervenes, it becomes a gesture that lacks compassion. An open microphone also becomes a lightning rod for histrionic teens (and many of these will attend another teenager's funeral, even if they didn't know the deceased). It's always better to select a few students who knew the deceased teen very well. Their comments are often genuine and healing.

Remarks or Shared Memories. Selected friends and family members should provide this portion of the service. Their remarks should be about five to seven minutes long and well thought out because the service can get emotional. Make sure you coordinate the content of all are eulogizing the deceased so people aren't telling the same story. These short eulogies can be spaced throughout the ceremony.

Specific Ethnic or Family Rituals. As mentioned earlier, people may incorporate their ethnic customs into a funeral service. For example, in early African American funerals, it was customary to have flower girls escort the coffin along with the pallbearers. Some ethnic funerals require mourners to weep and wail loudly, symbolizing their love for the deceased. Others require mourners to carry candles. It's important the officiant coordinates these details with the family. You may ask, "Are there any family or traditional rituals your family expects to be a part of the ceremony?"

Personal Touches. Typically there is little time to craft some personal touches, unless the teen died of a terminal illness. However, these can include displays of poems and writings and artwork by the teen, playing songs that were written or recorded by the deceased, and a video slideshow or pictorial presentation of the life and accomplishments of the deceased. In addition, family members may request certain elements to reflect the life of the teen. For example, I've watched families bury teenage guys in their sports jerseys, and the deceased's teammates took part in the service by serving as pallbearers. Having artifacts (sports equipment, stuffed animals, journals, musical instruments, and so on) in or near the coffin is not uncommon.

Flowers. Flowers are a part of the funeral tradition in just about every culture—some requiring more than others. But many times a family will establish a fund with a charitable organization (in the teenager's name) and ask people to make monetary donations in lieu of flowers. A youth worker may be asked for suggestions regarding where those charitable donations can be directed. If there is a need in the youth ministry it is not inappropriate to suggest that funds be directed there when so asked. Make sure your church leaders sign off on your suggestion before you make it.

3.2E SAMPLE CEREMONIES

The following are just templates or frameworks that can help you begin planning a ceremony:

Funeral or Memorial Service. This service remembers the life of the deceased and focuses on the hope of the believer. It can be a bittersweet time of sorrow and celebration.

Prelude Music.

Processional. The officiant, family, and pallbearers may elect to file in after guests are seated. If this isn't done, the family may be seated before guests arrive. They may greet the family with condolences, similar to the setting created at the wake.

Invocation. The officiant recognizes the solemnity of this gathering, acknowledges the grief and joy (in the light of a "home-going" for the loved one of a Christian family), and then prays for God's comfort and blessing.

Special Music. This can be interjected throughout the service.

Eulogy. This should be done first by the officiant, who gives factual details and a memory of significant characteristics of the deceased.

Scripture Reading.

Shared Memories by Friends and Family. Many people may be involved in this element of the ceremony. They can speak successively, but it makes more of an impact and offers more healing if they're spread throughout the remainder of the service.

Homily. A homily is a short (10-minute) devotional or talk. This should focus on the hope of the Christian in the light of death. The homily should not be a come-to-Jesus-fire-and-brimstone opportunistic sermon that exploits death. The truth of the gospel can be powerfully communicated in Christian hope. This positive short devotional can both comfort grieving believers and create a hunger in unbelievers, who have no hope.

Recessional. In the event there's an open casket, guests are given an opportunity to once again file past the casket and offer condolences to the family. If the casket is closed, it can be wheeled out ceremonially with the pallbearers and family following it. Then the guests are dismissed as well. In the event of a memorial service, the family may elect to form a receiving line to receive the condolences of guests. This is often done near the site where memorabilia from the deceased is displayed.

Interment or Committal Service. This is very short and done at the gravesite. The family may be seated, but the guests will stand for this brief ceremony.

Gravesite Remarks. These can go something like this:

> "We have come here to recognize this as the final resting place for *(deceased's name)*'s body. Scripture reminds us that our bodies were made of dust and they'll return to dust. But for the believer, the story doesn't end in burial. We know that someday Christ will resurrect us in bodily form with a new body, free from pain, sickness, and sorrow. We also know that while we await that day, those who've preceded us in death are in the presence of Jesus, more joyful and alive than we are now. We look forward to that day when we are reunited with *(deceased's name)* and our Lord Jesus Christ."

Scripture Reading.

Closing Prayer of Comfort for Family and Friends.

Dismissal of Guests. The funeral director often does this by saying, "This concludes our funeral and committal services." If there is a reception following, then the details are announced at this time.

3.3 HELPING SURVIVING TEENAGERS

While we've talked about the stages of grief, it's important to mention again that teens work through their grief in different ways and at different paces. The process may become more complicated as psychological factors are added. For example, teens can be a bit more prepared when a peer dies from illness. They're able to work through the impending loss by doing some advance grieving. But when a teen dies suddenly because of an accident, those left behind must not only deal with the loss, but also work through the psychological trauma that accompanies a tragic death. They may play out different scenarios in their minds and experience the trauma repeatedly. This becomes even more complicated when the death was violent or involved multiple teen deaths.

3.3A HELPING A GRIEVING TEENAGER

When teenagers encounter death, their primary need is the love and support of significant caregivers, and the youth worker is often on the front lines in those students' lives. The following are some helpful tips you should keep in mind as you minister to hurting teenagers.

Listen. When a teenager is grieving, this isn't the time to view the conversation as a teachable moment. You don't need to correct his perceptions or theology, nor do you need to give advice. You need to quietly and attentively listen to him.

Ask open-ended and clarifying questions. It's important that students process the emotions surrounding death. Open-ended questions can't be answered with a yes or no. Yet, a question like, "How are you doing?" is not an open-ended question because it solicits a single-word answer, such as, "Okay" or, "Fine." Instead, ask something like, "What emotions have you felt in the last 24 hours?" As the student talks, you can ask clarifying questions to help you and the student process the trauma of death. Death provokes many emotions, as we've already discussed, so be aware it may take a while for the teen to process them.

Be aware of gender differences in teens' reactions to death. Guys tend to hold things in and respond out of anger. Give guys permission to cry, meaning you should acknowledge it's okay for them to cry. Provide a safe environment for guys to be emotional. In other words, don't have this conversation in the middle of a coffee shop. Realize that guys may act indifferent or unaffected because they process their emotions differently than girls do or they need to save face.

Acknowledge teenagers' feelings. Teens may have never encountered death this close before, and they may be confused by a rush of different emotions. Your acknowledgment of their feelings will give them a point of reference. They'll begin to understand there isn't a right or wrong way to grieve. Many times teens feel guilt or helplessness when a traumatic death occurs. This may be a good place to start.

Be available. You may need to pursue a teen as a way of making yourself available. Therefore, making calls or texting students until the trauma has passed may be your primary ministry objective. Remember, grief is fatiguing, so teens may not take the initiative. Also remember that the closer the teen is to the trauma or the person who died, the more affected or even at risk they are.

Watch for the emotional avalanche effect. Teens feel corollary pain and hurt when others grieve. Death and grief may also reopen old emotional wounds that haven't healed properly. This can be exhausting for the youth worker because it may appear the teen is histrionic. Acknowledge the teenager's pain, help her separate it from the grief of death, and establish a time when you can talk about her other issues in the weeks to come. You may also want to refer a student to a professional counselor.

Encourage teens to seek help. They should get support from as many people as they can, so arrange to have a variety of people available to them 24/7 (teachers, counselors, medical professionals, pastoral caregivers, parents, and friends).

Be okay with silence. Take the grieving teenager for a walk and just sit quietly with her. Don't push her to talk. When she's ready, she'll open up. Provide comfort and support without being overbearing. Remind him that while his grief, pain, and suffering are unique to him, others have been down the same road. Grief and sorrow strike many, and many survive. Assure teenagers it's healing to talk, but you can wait until they are ready. Note: You must also realize that a teenager may not want to talk to you. Some teens are funny like that. If this is the case, don't take it personally (and if you do, find someone to talk to). But encourage students to talk to an adult, not just to their peers.

Allow teens to ask questions. They may have a range of inquiries, from factual questions regarding the death of their friend or loved one to questions about faith and eternity. Many times their questions can be emotionally loaded. Be calm, honest, and straightforward. If you have an answer, give it. If you don't know the answer but you can find out, say that. If you just don't know the answer, then acknowledge that, too. Talking through a teenager's questions may provide a great time for you to be transparent and talk through your personal faith process.

Maintain as much life continuity and normalcy as possible. Encourage teens to eat, exercise, come to youth group, and do other things that are routines in their day. They may not want to, but they need to—especially in the first weeks following the initial trauma and funeral. Participating in these activities will help teens understand that life continues. Keep in mind that the fatigue that accompanies grief can render teenagers lethargic to daily routine, including decision making. You may need to come alongside fatigued and grieving teenagers (or coach their parents to do so) and help them do what they need to do.

Prepare teens for a wake and funeral. Some students may have never been to one. Tell them they'll see the body of their dead friend or loved one. Explain that it will be emotional for them and for many people. Assure them it's okay to be emotional. Assure them there will be plenty of people there to support them. Some teens may have some fears about seeing their friend or loved one in the state of death. If for any reason teens don't want to go to a wake or funeral, talk through those emotions with them. Gently point out they don't have to go, but that they may later regret not going.

Share memories of the deceased, including funny stories. Remember that humor and laughter are healing.

Explain that grief is a process. Teach grieving teenagers that grief is a process that will end, but it takes a while. Forewarn teens that they may feel pain or sorrow when they hear certain songs that remind them of the deceased, or when anniversary dates come up (birthday, prom, holidays, and so on).

Relieve a teenager of the burden of adult responsibilities. It's common for adolescents who lose a parent to take on roles before their readiness.

Assure teens that life continues. People don't "move on," they "continue on" with the routines of life. Don't minimize the loss and the huge hole that's been created, but accentuate the hope of continuation. Be aware that teens may fear forgetting the deceased. Remind them they have pictures of their friend and suggest they jot down any stories they can remember so they don't forget—and so life will continue with the security of remembrance.

Help them experience closure. Students may make a comment such as, "I wish I had said _____ or done _____." If this is the case, then give them the opportunity to gain closure by using an empty chair. Encourage grieving students to say whatever they need to say, but to do so to an empty chair, as though their friend is sitting there. If closure requires action, like something the teen wishes had been done, then have the student identify a representative (the deceased's younger sibling, parent, or significant friend) and carry out the action.

Encourage grieving teens to minister to others. Serving people helps them put their pain in perspective and draws from the healing power that accompanies giving. It also changes the teen's perspective from being self-absorbed to other centered.

Keep close tabs on kids with a history of rebellion. Pain often causes rebellious students to act out. Or they believe it gives them license to be reckless. You may have to call them on this and help them engage in positive behaviors to deal with the pain.

(We'll discuss this more in section 3.3C.) Be loving, firm, and direct while verbalizing your expectations and boundaries for the rebellious teen: "Don't drive fast and reckless because you're angry, don't drink, don't fight...". Encourage parents to do the same for their teenagers.

Help teens manage the changes that come with death. They may have to adjust some of their routines, family schedules, and social contexts. Talk about how this will be different, what they plan to do, and what kind of help they need to change.

Model healthy grieving and coping skills. Self-disclose—tell students what you're thinking and feeling. Let them see and participate in your sorrow. Tell them that this tragedy raises questions you find frustrating and unanswerable, too. Show them what you do to overcome grief and how you plan to readjust with a life that continues.

3.3B DEBRIEFING A YOUTH GROUP

The first time a youth group meets following the death of a teenager, the gathering needs to be structured to address the students' grief. This is not the time to continue with a teaching series or maintain routine activity. The entire time should be dedicated to the care of the youth group. This is important because it will accomplish the following:

- It helps teens see death in the context of a faith community and grapple with a theology of death.
- It gives teens a safe place to grieve with and console each other.
- It surfaces complicated grief issues in teens, meaning that teens who may have greater difficulty dealing with death will show signs of deeper mental health issues. The death of a teenager can

become the catalyst to bring into the open issues other teens face. This can allow the youth worker to mobilize resources for those teens and maybe prevent another tragic experience.

There are some things that you must do in preparation for this debriefing:

Make sure all volunteers and adult supporters are briefed. Have them arrive about 45 minutes before the meeting starts. They should know what you're going to say to students and what resources are available, and they should be coached to scatter throughout the group of teens so they can console and intervene if a student needs help. Make sure you give them permission to grieve with students. They may feel the need to hide their own sorrow for fear of not ministering effectively.

Communicate your plans to parents. You can do this via email, a posting on a Web page, or through a phone chain. Let parents know you'll be dealing with the death of the student. Give them the facts and allow them to be involved, if they desire. Parents should not be encouraged to come to this meeting, out of sensitivity to your students. You don't want it to turn into a "show" where teens feel like they're being watched or can't be themselves. Tell parents you have a crisis team who will be available to students during the meeting and in the days following. If a parent insists on attending, then allow them to do so by remaining on the periphery of the room, ready to assist if you need their help. In your communication with parents, coach them to be sensitive and available to their teens afterward; to drop off and pick up their teens before and after this meeting, if they feel the need to do so; to be available to grieve with and listen to their teenagers and acknowledge the sorrow of death; and to monitor their own teenager's well-being.

Have a crisis team available. It's my recommendation every youth ministry have a crisis team waiting in the wings and prepared to come to the aid of students as needed. Oftentimes the death of a teenager is the impetus to form such a team. These people should be at your debriefing to immediately lend their expertise, if necessary. Members of this team should include—

- Clinical counselors or mental health professionals. This could also include school counselors, psychiatric nurses, or social workers from your congregation. These people aren't coming to do therapy; they're just there to assist if needed.
- Medical professionals. In the event a student becomes ill, passes out, or the trauma triggers some other physical problem (like a seizure), a doctor, physician's assistant, nurse, or paramedic should be available.
- Pastoral caregivers. Many churches have people who are trained in pastoral care programs like Stephen Ministries (www.ste phenministries.org).
- Teachers. These people have some connectedness to teenagers in your community. Teachers in your congregation can continue to keep a watchful eye on grieving kids while they're at school.
- Community leaders. If the death of a student is homicide-related, you might ask a police spokesperson to be available to answer questions within the confines of any information that isn't privileged. They can also help dispel student's fears. Other community leaders may include members of the board of education, youth advocates, and parachurch youth ministry leaders.
- Parents and grandparents. It's good to select a few loving couples (parent- and grandparent-aged) to be on this team. They can be parents to parentless kids, as well as an extension of parents within a church family.

Secure a warm and inviting environment. Make sure there's plenty of room so students can move around to console one another, huddle together, or sit in silence. Students may desire, and should be allowed to, sit on the floor, sit in chairs, lie down, stand, or engage in any posture their grief demands. Have plenty of tissues and water available.

Be honest about the purpose of this meeting. Students must know ahead of time that this event is dedicated to talking about the tragedy of the death of their peer(s). Realize that the routine of their lives has already been disrupted by death. Giving them a heads-up helps them not be caught off guard again. It may also be a time when hurting teens who aren't a part of your ministry will come to get help.

There are a number of elements you should incorporate into the actual meeting time. I've listed them in an order that might help you implement the meeting:

- Acknowledge the solemnity of the occasion and pray that God will bring healing, comfort, and hope to the family and friends who've been touched by this tragedy.
- Give students the facts of the events surrounding the death. This should follow suit with your prepared statement. Tell students you have clearance from the family (or families) involved to say what you did. They need to know and understand boundaries.
- Answer any questions they may have. Acknowledge that you may not be allowed to answer some questions because of the privacy afforded the family, because of privileged information, or because you don't know the answer to their question.
- Move into the most important part of the meeting—the time when students get to talk. If you feel comfortable doing so,

pass this section off to a trained counselor. If no counselor is available, then you'll need to facilitate this time. Explain they need to talk about what they're feeling and thinking. Let students know that this will take up the majority of your time together, but there are ground rules:

- Respect each other because everyone processes terrible news differently.
- Feelings aren't right or wrong, and students are allowed to feel here. Caution them they may feel very angry (which is acceptable), but how they express that anger must be appropriate and consistent with keeping this room a safe place.
- Acknowledge that it's also okay *not* to feel anything. Kids may wonder if that's abnormal. Remind them there is no "normal."
- Tell them that when someone is talking, others shouldn't interrupt. And the person who's talking should be sensitive that others may want to talk, too.
- Let them know who the other people in the room are (members of the crisis team) and that these adults are here to offer their support and care and to grieve with them.
- Let them know it's okay to share a funny memory and that humor is often very healing.
- Tell them they can share as often as they want or not at all. If the group is very large, encourage them to get into smaller groups and talk.

- After you've laid the ground rules, allow students to talk—they'll share stories, memories, personal struggles with the death, and humorous anecdotes. If this is slow to begin, then you should start things off. Let them be emotive and console each other.

- Bring closure by talking about God as our Comforter and Hope. This should not be an opportunity to sermonize, nor should it be long and wordy. Take about five to seven minutes to put things into a theological context.
- Open the door that students may have spiritual questions. Tell them they can raise those questions at any time and you and the other adult leaders will be available to talk through those spiritual questions with them whenever they're ready. Many times those types of questions will come up days later.
- In addition, keep in mind that if a teenager is going to be spiritually impacted by another teen's death, it usually comes about as a result of any spiritual questioning that takes place after the initial shock and grieving are past. Therefore, be sensitive to that process without confronting teens into making spiritual decisions.
- Make sure teens know this isn't the end of the grief process, but it's an "open door" to continue to work through their grief. Remind students that there are resources and people available to help them.
- Pray for and with the students.
- Allow students to stay as long as they like and continue to talk. This is often when you need to have your crisis team available. Many students who have complicated grief issues tend to become overwhelmed and stay behind. Others may just find this a more intimate time to hang with friends.
- Make sure students who are leaving alone after the meeting are in a proper emotional state to drive. You may offer to follow them home or ask them to call their parents, notifying them they are on their way home. If you believe that the teen is not emotionally fit to get behind the wheel of the car then treat it the same way you would a drunk driver: Take them home or call parents to come and pick them up.

After the initial meeting, create times and opportunities for teens to be together without agendas or program. Encourage parents to invite students into their homes. Encourage teens to organize their own meetings. Teenagers need a lot of hang-out time when death hits a youth group. The sense of community and connectedness heals students and fills the gap left by death.

3.3C POSITIVE WAYS TO EXPRESS GRIEF

Adolescents may need to express their grief in a more tangible, creative, and positive way. Being proactive in your own grief will model healthy coping skills and bring a sense of closure as the tasks come to an end. A youth worker can enable students to take positive action in processing their grief in the following ways:

Be an active part in planning a memorial. Get clearance from the family on this and then craft a tribute from the youth group to the deceased.

Create a memorial Web page. Often the deceased's MySpace or Facebook page becomes a memorial as people leave their condolences. But it may be a good idea to craft a separate Web page that has the unique signature of the youth group on it. Then link their personal MySpace or Facebook page to your church Web site. (Again, get the family's permission before doing so.)

Plant a memorial tree or garden on the church grounds. As the tree grows, it becomes a reminder of the life of not only the deceased individual, but also the principle of spiritual deep-rooted growth those in the youth group must continue to have. Scripture often uses the analogy of a tree firmly planted to illustrate spiritual life and growth.

Create a photo wall or collage in the youth room. If this is meant to be more permanent, buy a large frame and create the collage to fill the frame. Then have a calligrapher scribe an epitaph somewhere in the collage.

Journal. There are some grief journals on the market that are designed to help students write out their thoughts, feelings, and memories. Or you might encourage students to bypass the journal and write the same information and ideas in a blog. This may also be set up as a page on a memorial Web site.

Create a book of memories. Suggest that students write stories, letters, and poems that serve as a reminder of the deceased. Then assemble them into one booklet and have them bound and reprinted. The youth group can then present the book to the parents or loved one of the deceased.

Fund-raise and erect a monument. This becomes an ambitious undertaking and is best suited if a youth group suffers the loss of a beloved youth worker. I've seen churches display everything from bronze garden statues of Christ to commemorative bells. This type of memorial must be researched, commissioned, and sanctioned by the church. But it's often done.

Make a wall banner or quilt to hang in the youth room. Many times this is done using the clothing of the departed teen. Students can write memories, qualities, quotations, and so on, on blank squares that make up the quilt. If the group raises money for the project, then a professional could be hired to embroider the squares, giving the quilt a more polished look.

Homemade jewelry. A youth group may make wristbands or necklaces as a memorial to a deceased friend.

Participate in the Kindness Project. This is a program whereby a youth group can engage in some anonymous and random act of kindness in honor of the deceased teen. The details can be obtained through the MISS Foundation at their Web site: http://www.miss foundation.org/kindness/index.html.

3.3D COMMON MISTAKES YOUTH WORKERS MAKE

There are some common mistakes youth workers make with grieving teens and families. Remember, you're there to help and serve *them*. Too often a well-meaning youth worker's need to be needed kicks in and the focus shifts. So here's a list of don'ts you should note:

Don't be overbearing. Spending time with them daily, even for an extended period, may not be bad. But hovering is another story. Get a read from family members, and when in doubt—ask. You can say, "I realize there may be a lot of people who are trying to help or are coming over to your home. I want to be available, but I don't want to be overbearing, either. So I'll plan the following *(fill in the blank)*, and you let me know if that's okay with you."

Don't use Christian clichés. Many times these are comments that pop out when we don't know what else to say. So many of the clichés are true, but it's more appropriate for those to be a part of your heartfelt response *after* you've patiently listened, loved, and grieved with someone.

Don't look for teachable moments. This is not an opportunity to show your theological correctness. I've watched many youth workers make comments like, "God has allowed this so that many more can come to him." Statements like this only add insult to injury. And some have even used this as an opportunity to correct someone regarding a deceased person's eternal state, saying, "Well if your grandfather didn't receive Christ, then he probably isn't in heaven." Tactless and coldhearted—even if you believe this to be true—it's inappropriate to exercise your theological rightness in the face of a grieving individual.

Don't be afraid to ask. Many times youth workers avoid asking someone who's grieving how she feels and what she thinks, fearing they'll make the person emotional or hurt more. This isn't true; you may be the only one who's asking. In addition, don't be afraid to ask teens (when they give you verbal cues or you get a feeling in your gut) if *they're* thinking of dying, too. Some fear that asking a question like that may put ideas in a teenager's head—it doesn't. But it just may be the thing that prevents another tragedy.

Don't offer false reassurances and promises on behalf of God. This is often done during a terminal illness. But then when God doesn't answer the way we want him to or your assurance fails, the impact on the teen is even greater.

Don't hide your personal sorrow and grief. Remember, Jesus wept at the tomb of Lazarus in front of many onlookers.

Don't be melodramatic and sappy. I once observed a youth worker debriefing a youth group after a teenager's death. And when the group wasn't demonstrating enough pain and sorrow, the youth worker began emotionally manipulating the teenagers. Making comments like, "We'll never be together here on earth again" is melodramatic and provokes a different response from, "Someday we'll be reunited in heaven with our loved ones." Both say the same thing—only one is emotionally manipulative.

3.3E DEBRIEFING A VOLUNTEER STAFF

At some point it's important to debrief your staff apart from the youth. They may need to express their own grief over the loss of a student and the pain they feel from having shouldered the pain of the students they love and are passionate about. It's also good for them to find consolation in their peers and not students. Your debriefing process can follow the same plan as your debriefing of the youth group. I recommend that you do this twice—the first time as a briefing before they meet with students. During this time you can also give them pointers on how to minister to hurting teens. Then you should debrief your staff after the meeting with the students so your leaders can release the sorrow they bear on behalf of the youth.

3.3F MISCELLANEOUS TIPS

Provide resources and support tips for parents on the youth group's Web site or a handout. This may include tips on how parents can care for their grieving teenager.

If you can get professional counselors to donate their time have an open house or after-school drop-in time when students can come by and talk. Make sure parents know this is available.

Have students brainstorm ways they can support other grieving students who may not have any support system.

If the death of a student is extremely tragic, realize that the media may approach the students in your youth group for their reactions. While you can't keep the media away from students 24/7, you *can* keep them away from your meetings and church grounds. Realize that some students will look for their "15 minutes of fame." Advise students to be sensitive; ask parents and students to direct all media inquiries to a church spokesperson for more details.

A teenager's grief may be compounded in the months after the funeral. This comes from the realization of what's been lost and what's now different. And teenagers who lose a parent suddenly face a compounded grief because they also lose the gestures of loving care that parents provide.

3.4 DEALING WITH PERSONAL GRIEF

Like everyone else, you initially respond to grief in the same way. If the news is tragic, you initially meet it with shock and disbelief, just like Pastor Dave did at the beginning of this book. But almost immediately, you switch to pastor-mode. So there's often no time for you to process a tragedy and its impact on you. Certainly the death of a student will impact you, but your focus is on the needs, comfort, and available ministry to others who are hurting. Sooner or later, the grief surrounding the tragic death of someone you're close to will become personal. So how should a youth pastor deal with personal grief?

DECIDE TO GRIEVE

We have to realize that the shock we feel may be God's anesthetic for us. Most people follow shock with immense pain; but for a minister, the decisions that follow shock are to hold off the grief and control, protect, bring healing to, and console hurting survivors. This means that at some point we must revisit that initial shock and decide to grieve. That conscious choice is often difficult because it may come long after those around you have resolved their own grief. If you decide to stay in pastor-mode, then you'll deal with your grief in a very unhealthy way. Take time to stop being the pastor and do your own grief work.

ALLOW YOURSELF TO BE EMOTIONAL
Being emotionless or "keeping it under control" is not a sign of strength. Many leaders believe that if they show emotion in front of hurting people, they'll lose their credibility to help. This isn't true. Jesus modeled this for us when he wept over Lazarus in front of so many people. Sometimes people don't need our answers—they need our tears, and not because we're being an example to them. When we genuinely hurt in the context of a loving community, we have the opportunity to experience the healing grace and wonderful hope of a powerful God. On the other hand, remember that grief is a process, so if you don't feel the intense sorrow others feel—avoid self-inflicted guilt trips. Grief will come in its time and place. Just don't ignore it when it does.

FACING THE SENSELESSNESS OF DEATH
While we know death is inevitable and universal, we can never find an answer that satisfies. From the moment you receive a call about someone's death, you realize that one of the dimensions of being a pastor is that you serve as an answer man. This can be frustrating and shallow for you! When C. S. Lewis contemplated the pain, loss, and senselessness of death, he couldn't find the answers. He wondered where God was in the midst of the pain and why God didn't answer. Lewis wasn't fearful he was going to abandon his belief in God, but rather that he'd conclude that

God was absent, distant, and uninterested. Like the story of Job from the Bible, we can't fully understand the ways of God, and we must learn to trust him. This is much easier to say than it is to live out. We must come to a place where we realize that answers don't heal the heart—hope does. Grief begins to heal when we become overwhelmed with the hope of eternity, of being protected by a powerful Savior, of being reunited with departed loved ones, of knowing that the deceased believer is currently more alive, joyful, and pain-free than we are.

TALK TO SOMEONE

At some point you'll need to stop and process all the events surrounding the death. Talk through your feelings of being in that hospital room or at that gravesite or telling your students the news. Share your deepest feelings. Talk about your relationship with the deceased student and the family. Realize that God works through you to minister to others because God has chosen to pour his love and grace through you. Then realize you're not the exception to the rule. God will choose others to help you heal as well. If you grieve alone, then you prolong the process and miss the love and care of a gracious God.

SEEK PROFESSIONAL HELP

Sometimes the grief process can be too overwhelming. I know many youth workers who are great ministers, and when they encounter death they just kick it into gear and do the job. However, months later they find themselves overwhelmed because they owned and carried the pain of so many others. They couldn't get past the grief. When this occurs, it's time for a mental health checkup. A brief series of therapy sessions can help you sort things out and prevent you from losing your effectiveness.

RESOURCES ON TEENAGERS AND DEATH
| SECTION 4 |

4.1 AGENCIES

Most agencies are local. Many hospitals network with hospice services that offer or have access to teen support groups.

Alcohol Poisoning Hotline: If the person is unconscious, call 9-1-1 or your local emergency number. If the person is conscious, call 800-222-1222 and you'll be automatically routed to your local poison control center for instructions or directions to the nearest hospital.

The Compassionate Friends: The mission of The Compassionate Friends is to assist families toward the positive resolution of grief following the death of a child (of any age) and to provide information to help others be supportive. You can find support in your area from their Web site: *www.compassionatefriends.org*

GriefShare: This is an international program that trains leadership and offers support groups. To locate a group and access their resources go to *www.griefshare.org*

Open Directory Project: This Web page may be a start for finding a nearby support group. It lists a number of groups in various states and the U.K. and offers a description of each group: *www. dmoz.org/Health/Mental_Health/Grief,_Loss_and_Bereavement/ Support_Groups*

Youth for Christ: The GrievingTeens Program has resources and guides to start or participate in support groups in retreat and camp contexts. They also offer great online resources, printed materials, seminars, and consulting. Contact them at:
YFC GrievingTeens
PO Box 14370
Palm Desert, California 92255
grievingteens@gmail.com.
Materials and more information can be accessed from *http:// yfcgrievingteens.org*

4.2 ONLINE RESOURCES

www.bereavedparents.com
Bereaved Parents offers forums, chat rooms, and other resources for parents who've lost a child.

www.stop-the-choking-game.com
The G.A.S.P. (Games Adolescents Shouldn't Play) Web site takes preventative measures to encourage teens to stop playing or allowing their friends to play choking games. There are also downloadable educational materials available on this site.

www.growthhouse.org
Growth House Inc. provides a Web site with resources for life-threatening illnesses and end-of-life care. Its mission is to "improve the quality of compassionate care for people who are dying

through public education and global professional collaboration." They have more than 4,000 pages of high-quality full-text education content on end-of-life care provided by more than 30 collaborating members.

www.groww.org/Branches/guiding2.htm
This is an online chat room for grieving teenagers. The chat is hosted by an adult, and times are posted as to when the chat is available. The Web site is a bit difficult to navigate, but teens can do it.

www.last-memories.com
This Web site provides free resources to create your own online memorial page. It may be a great place to direct students who need to process their grief creatively.

www.massgeneral.org/children/adolescenthealth/articles/aa_terminal_illness.aspx
MassGeneral Hospital for Children's Web page gives insight into teens who face terminal illness.

www.mayoclinic.com/health/alcohol-poisoning/DS00861/DSECTION=3
This is the Mayo Clinic's page about the effects of alcohol poisoning.

www.cancer.gov/cancertopics/youngpeople
This site belongs to the National Cancer Institute. They have an online resource entitled "Young People with Cancer: A Handbook for Parents," which answers a lot of questions parents and kids

may have. The resource also coaches parents in defining effective care strategies.

www.stephenministries.org
Stephen Ministries provides grief recovery training and resources.

4.3 BOOKS AND PRINTED MATERIALS
Better Safe Than Sued: Keeping Your Students and Ministry Alive by Jack Crabtree (Zondervan/Youth Specialties, 2008). This is a book written to youth pastors and churches about preventative measures that can be taken to keep teens safe from tragedy, among other things.

Fire in My Heart, Ice in My Veins: A Journal for Teenagers Experiencing a Loss by Enid Samuel Traisman (Centering Corporation, 1992). This is a journal designed to help teens navigate grief at their own pace and in a creative way.

A Grief Observed by C. S. Lewis (HarperCollins, 2001). This book may serve an older adolescent or youth worker well in working through grief. Lewis wrote this short book as a series of notes and journal entries after his wife died.

The Grieving Teen: A Guide for Teenagers and Their Friends by Helen Fitzgerald (Fireside, 2000). This book is very easy to read and very comprehensive. Fitzgerald is a grief therapist, and she coaches teens through the process of grief in this book.

Helping Teens Cope with Death by The Dougy Center for Grieving Children (The Dougy Center, 1999). This book offers advice to caregivers on how to support and determine when professional help is needed for bereaved teens.

Losing Someone You Love: When a Brother or Sister Dies by Elizabeth Richter (Putnam Juvenile, 1986). This book helps teenagers and young adults cope with the death of a sibling.

Straight Talk about Death with Teenagers: How to Cope with Losing Someone You Love by Earl Grollman (Beacon Press, 1993). This book is excellent for teens. Written from a theological perspective, it offers help, hope, and creative ways for teens to work through their grief.

Surviving the Death of a Child by John Munday and Frances Wohlenhaus-Munday (Westminster John Knox Press, 1995). This book is also written from a theological perspective to grieving parents.

Turn My Mourning into Dancing: Finding Hope in Hard Times by Henri Nouwen (Thomas Nelson, 2001). This book deals with a rich, contemplative theological look at grief and death. The book is great for youth workers and may serve a more mature teenager well.

NOTES

1. Centers for Disease Control and Prevention, "Teen Drivers: Fact Sheet," Motor Vehicle Safety page at CDC's Web site (updated January 26, 2009), http://www.cdc.gov/MotorVehicleSafety/Teen_Drivers/teendrivers_factsheet.html (accessed 3/14/09).

2. Richard P. Compton and Patricia Ellison-Potter, *Teen Driver Crashes: A Report to Congress*, July 2008, National Highway Traffic Safety Administration (2008), http://nhtsa.gov/staticfiles/DOT/NHTSA/Traffic%20Injury%20Control/Articles/Associated%20Files/811005.pdf (accessed 3/14/09).

3. Centers for Disease Control and Prevention, "Research Update—The Choking Game: CDC's Findings on a Risky Youth Behavior," Home & Recreational Safety page at CDC's Web site (updated January 19, 2009), http://www.cdc.gov/HomeandRecreationalSafety/Choking/choking_game.html (accessed 3/14/09).

4. G.A.S.P.: Choking Game Community Support Web site, "Victims: Under 19" List, http://www.deadlygameschildrenplay.com/en/stats-statistics.asp (accessed 3/14/09). Also see http://www.stop-the-choking-game.com/en/home.html for more information about G.A.S.P.

5. Centers for Disease Control and Prevention, "Unintentional Strangulation Deaths from the 'Choking Game' Among Youths Aged 6–19 Years—United States, 1995–2007," *Morbidity and Mortality Weekly Report 57*, no. 6 (February 15, 2008): 141-144, http://www.cdc.gov/mmwr/preview/mmwrhtml/mm5706a1.htm (accessed 3/14/09).

6. Centers for Disease Control and Prevention, "The Choking Game: Risky Youth Behavior," CDC Features page at CDC's Web site (updated February 25, 2008), http://www.cdc.gov/Features/ChokingGame/ (accessed 3/14/09).

7. Donna Leinwand, "Kohl's and Target drop drinking games," USA Today (posted 1/10/2007), http://www.usatoday.com/news/nation/2007-01-10-drinkgames_x.htm (accessed 3/14/09).

8. National Advisory Council on Alcohol Abuse and Alcoholism, Task Force on College Drinking, "Facts About Alcohol Poisoning," College Drinking: Changing the Culture Web site (last reviewed 7/11/2007), http://www.collegedrinkingprevention.gov/OtherAlcoholInformation/factsAboutAlcoholPoisoning.aspx (accessed 3/14/09).

9. David R. Freyer, "Care of the Dying Adolescent: Special Considerations," Pediatrics 113, no. 2 (February 2004): 381-388, http://pediatrics.aappublications.org/cgi/content/full/113/2/381%20 (accessed 3/14/09).

10. Cystic Fibrosis Foundation, "What is the life expectancy for people who have CF (in the United States)?" Frequently Asked Questions page of the CFF Web site (updated 5/15/07), http://www.cff.org/AboutCF/Faqs/#What_is_the_life_expectancy_for_people_who_have_CF_(in_the_United_States)? (accessed 3/14/09).

11. Centers for Disease Control and Prevention, "Slide 8: Reported AIDS Cases among Adolescents 13 to 19 Years of Age, by Sex, 1985-2006," HIV/AIDS Surveillance in Adolescents and Young Adults (through 2006), (last modified May 21, 2008), http://www.cdc.gov/hiv/topics/surveillance/resources/slides/adolescents/index.htm (accessed 3/14/09).

12. H. C. Kung, D. L. Hoyert, J. Xu, and S. L. Murphy, "Deaths: Final Data for 2005," National Vital Statistics Report 56, no. 10 (2008), http://www.cdc.gov/nchs/data/nvsr/nvsr56/nvsr56_10.pdf (accessed 3/14/09).

13. Elisabeth Kübler-Ross, On Death and Dying: What the Dying Have to Teach Doctors, Nurses, Clergy, and Their Own Families (New York: Simon and Schuster, 1997).

14. Ibid., 265.

15. National Conference of Commissioners on Uniform State Laws, "Uniform Determination of Death Act," Annual Conference Meeting July 26–August 1, 1980, http://www.law.upenn.edu/bll/archives/ulc/fnact99/1980s/udda80.htm (accessed 3/14/09).

16. Catholic Book Publishing Company, Order of Christian Funerals, trans. The International Commission on English in the Liturgy (Totowa, New Jersey: Catholic Book Publishing Company, 1999).

CPSIA information can be obtained at www.ICGtesting.com
Printed in the USA
LVOW130948201012

303717LV00002B/7/P